EASTBOURNE
Building A Duke's Dream

TO SEE ALL OF ALEX ASKAROFF'S BOOKS
CURRENTLY AVAILABLE
VISIT AMAZON

Crows Nest Publications:
BK1 Patches Of Heaven: ISBN 0-9539410-4-3
BK2 Skylark Country: ISBN 0-9539410-2-7
BK3 High Streets & Hedgerows: ISBN 0-9539410-3-5
Tales From The Coast: ISBN 978 0-9539410-5-6
Norman, A Journey Through Time: ISBN 978-0-9539410-6-3

Fireship Press, Arizona, USA:
Sussex Born And Bred: ISBN 978-1-935585-22-0
Corner Of The Kingdom: ISBN 978-1-61179-067-2

Amazon Books:
A fairy tale, Gizzleink, Why The Best Fireworks Sparkled.
ISBN: 978-1-500185-60-2
The Magic Sewing Machine: 978-1-910489-57-4

Country Books, UK:
Have I Got A Story For You: ISBN 978-1-906789-85-5
Isaac Singer The First Capitalist: ISBN 978-1-910489-05-5
Glory Days: ISBN 978-1-910489-43-7

EASTBOURNE
Building A Duke's Dream

ALEX ASKAROFF

COUNTRY BOOKS

First Edition

Published by

Country Books, Courtyard Cottage, Little Longstone, Bakewell, Derbyshire DE45 1NN
Tel: 01629 640670

ISBN 978-1-910489-70-3 (paperback)

ISBN 978-1-910489-71-0 (hardback)

Printed in Great Britain by

4edge Ltd., 22 Eldon Way, Eldon Way Industrial Estate, Hockley, Essex SS5 4AD
Tel: 01702 200243

The William Terriss Memorial Lifeboat House, along the promenade, was opened by Her Grace the Duchess of Devonshire on 16 July 1898. The James Stevens No 6 lifeboat was the first lifeboat to be housed at the station. On November 8th 1902 the SS Southport, out of Cardiff, ran into difficulties near Hastings. In a fierce gale the James Stevens was launched with a double bank of oars to tackle the huge waves. The fearless crew helped in yet another successful mission. Out of the 17 men that made up the crew no less than eight were members of the Erridge family.

George John Erridge
The Erridge Family seem to have been here as long as the South Downs.
Here is George John 'Quack' Erridge looking every inch the boatman he was.

I am proud to be listed among the many old family names of Eastbourne in this
passionate tale of our town.
Chris George Erridge 2019

ACKNOWLEDGEMENTS

It would be impossible to write such a book as this without all the people who have gone before who took the time to document and photograph our history. It is with much gratitude that I thank them all.

Our remaining local libraries were a wonderful source of information, as was The Eastbourne Heritage Centre and Town Hall. The Internet provided as much information as disinformation. I am starting to understand that I need to have a big bowl of salt ready every time I go online for dates, Facts and figures. Many online sources need a big pinch of it!

My big thanks go to so many of the local fishing families who have donated their time, stories, photos and insights, from the Chesters to the Allchorns, Erridges, Prodgers, Pococks, and Bonifaces. Chris Erridge has been a mine of information and images, thanks mate. Also to our own families of Cottingtons and Reeds, I mention many of them in the following pages.

A huge thank you to my dear friend David Arscott who has spent a lifetime writing about the area that he loves, producing many of my favourite books including, *A Century of Eastbourne*. His fascinating archives of early images has been deeply appreciated.

By far the best books I have ever read on the old fishing families of Eastbourne were written by Ted Hide, *The Fishermen of Eastbourne* and *The Pleasure Boatmen of Eastbourne*. Ted's roots lay deep in the soil and sea of the area, his family stretching back through the generations and centuries. Long before the town we know today existed the Hide family were here. Ted, Thank you, your help has been invaluable.

Thank you also to the Eastbourne Remembers Pavilion Café Exhibition in the summer of 2018 which helped with some amazing details. The National Maritime Museums in London and Cornwall, the Hastings Fishermen's Museum. The National Archives were a godsend. The RNLI Eastbourne Lifeboat Museum, Eastbourne Library, Eastbourne Herald, and the Eastbourne Heritage Centre. Finally, The Story of Eastbourne, in Terminus Road, had a great exhibition in the spring of 2019. They were a fantastic help with two missing pieces of information for my book.

Other images in this publication are by permission of Alex Askaroff, the people named in the book, or are in the public domain. I have tried to be as accurate as possible and hope that I have succeeded more than I have failed. If any copyright holder believes this is not the case we would be pleased to be informed to correct further editions.

AUTHOR'S NOTE

I must say a massive thank you to all my friends and family who put up with me rambling on about my projects. To Dick Richardson, my publisher at Country Books, who painstakingly builds them for me. A huge thank you to Corrinne, my favourite daughter in law in the whole world. This book has her magic touch. Thank you also to Malcolm Lawson who once again did the final read through. I did take note Malcolm (to most of it).

I have had great fun compiling and researching this story. I know it won't please everyone, the academics will say there is not enough detail and too much story. My regular readers will say there is not enough story and too much detail. So I have braced myself hoping that the good will outweigh the bad. This is a story that needed to be put down for posterity and I hope that you will read and enjoy it with the same enthusiasm as it was written.

ALEX ASKAROFF

DEDICATION

In 2018 as if by magic two grandchildren appeared. Alena and Evelyn, this book is dedicated to you two, have a great life.

CONTENTS

INTRODUCTION

I have to start by telling you that this has been an astonishing book to write. I began it when I was in my thirties and I was still writing it in my sixties! How do you start a book about a new town that practically grew out of wastelands and cornfields? A town built by a Duke who pulled all the outlying settlements into one thriving community. A community that is still growing 140 years later?

I looked at all of the most important principles needed to build a town. I realised that long before the important buildings could go up, all the infrastructure needed to be in place. Not so easy when electricity did not even exist, gas was just getting started, and the nearest railway was miles away.

Eventually I struck gold, actually water. Of course water. It was the thread that joined the whole kit and caboodle, from the fishing hamlets where the fishermen plied their trade on the sea, to the fresh water needed for the new homes, to the very name of the town, 'East' of the river Bourne. It was the one strand that joined everything.

There was another problem. What should go between the covers and what to leave out? There was little chance of

1

including all the great Eastbourne properties and the history behind each one. Even if the Nazi's had damaged and destroyed nearly 11,000 in the Second World War! If I had, my book would turn into ten! I knew it was impossible to embrace them all.

The Grade II Eastbourne Heritage Centre for example, at 2 Carlisle Road, was built in 1876 to an amazing design by G A Wallis. It is an octagonal shaped building built on a sharp corner. The building was once the flag tower for Devonshire Baths (part of the Duke's Pleasure Grounds). It was known as Park Cottage. It was due to be demolished in 1978 but saved at the last moment. Vigorous appeals by the Eastbourne Civic Society, and fantastic fundraising by several groups saw it re-opened in 1985 by the 11th Duke of Devonshire. If ever you want to see a brilliantly designed multi-storey building perched on a piece of land the size of a postage stamp, take a close look at it.

Eastbourne Heritage Centre was once the Devonshire Baths flag tower.

My solution to the problem of what to include in my book was simple. Stick mainly to the impressive seafront properties that were part of the 7th Duke of Devonshire's plans when he decided to build a new town. The town we now call Eastbourne.

The name originally dates back to the 15th Century when it was decided to add 'East' to 'Bourne' to distinguish the growing hamlet as its own distinct area. The Eastbourne we know today was christened by the 7th Duke of Devonshire in the 1850's. His 'new town' had grown beyond all recognition from the original hamlet (which by then was just a small suburb of the new boomtown). Interestingly there is a legend that he was going to call his new town Burlington, as a memorial to his grandfather, the 1st Earl of Burlington. After the first massive hotel, The Burlington, had well publicised financial problems, the Duke changed his mind and selected Eastbourne for the name of his new town.

Also I was wondering, should I include the Canadians scaling the cliffs for their practice invasions during World War Two? Or the huge guns that lined the seafront and the men that manned them? What about the mined beaches and the barbed wire necklace that stretched along the coast to slow down an invading army? Or one of the first major communications cable to the continent? What about this, and what about that? There were so many rumours, legends and facts surrounding our area that it blows my mind. Even, as you will find out, a few ghosts, a witch, and a murder that shocked a nation!

Then I hit another problem. As I started this book each thread that I tugged was tied to twenty more. Take Ron Piper for example. His name would mean nothing to most people, but as a lad during the Second World War he was too young to enlist, yet old enough to join the Eastbourne Home Guard. He was instructed by the 'old boys', soldiers from the First World War, then handed a rifle. Ron and his buddy, Stan would patrol the seafront at night, keeping a keen eye out for the enemy. On their laborious journey they would stop and have a crafty smoke. As they chatted they would come up with various scenarios of just how they would stop the invading fleet with their huge arsenal of ten rounds of ammunition. When Ron asked his doddery old superior in the Home Guard what he should do if he saw the German Fleet, the reply was, "Idiot boy, run back and get the rest of us! We've got nine rifles and almost a hundred bullets!"

Luckily, Ron never had to find out what his crack squad of old men and children would have done against the might of the invading forces; but these stories are priceless. Incidentally, the Home Guard around Britain apparently shot 147 people between 1939 and 1945. The highest casualties being doctors on call! One person shot was actually a German, but whether the person was a spy or not I never managed to discover!

Stop reading now and get a refund if you are after a research book full of specific days and dates. This is going to be a good yarn packed with facts that will meander along like a lazy river in summertime. It is also going to be a book that you can hopefully quote for years to come.

You will find the following pages crammed with particulars like the ones above, some funny, some extraordinary, and all interesting. After writing so many books I soon discovered which ones sell. I can tell you from experience that if this covers its costs I will be astounded. However, after thirty years of collecting notes and researching my home town, my labour of love just had to be completed.

I swallowed my self-doubt and I hope that you will give me a little lenience over the coming pages and enjoy the characters that we meet. You may also learn some amazing details. It should prove to be an insight into bits of long forgotten Eastbourne, and a little of how our town (and even our country) grew into what we see today.

It was only in 2019 that it had all grown into a complete story. I can tell you one thing, you will never have read a book like it! Now, let's get started.

CHAPTER 1

This book will be a walk, a guide, and history lesson all in one as together we build Eastbourne. Everyone has walked the beautiful Eastbourne Promenade, one of the finest Victorian time capsules in the world but few have done the walk I am going to take you on.

The walk will be a short circular hike, probably no more than a mile or so. I am going to act as your tour guide, hopefully bringing Eastbourne to life with not only facts and figures, but tales from my boyhood, legends and history too.

You will notice that I mention water and Holywell countless times. There is a good reason for this. Besides the fact that water was one of the most important ingredients for the Duke's mix to make a perfect town, it was also one of his and his son's biggest problems.

We take water for granted today as it pours from our taps; clean, safe and ready to drink. However, for all of history pure water has been held in almost magical reverence. It is our most essential element of life. From Lourdes in France to St Columba's Well in Ireland, water is still revered and blessed for its miraculous healing properties. The story of water is as fascinating a tale that has ever been told, for it is really the story of human evolution.

Water, besides being the very essence of life itself, is forever entwined in the early history and the development of Eastbourne as a thriving town. And so our story of Eastbourne is also the story of how safe, clean water came to the masses.

The Romans loved this area; their buildings and remains are dotted everywhere, some of which we shall come across over the following pages. After the Dark Ages, the first detailed mention of the area that I can find is in the *Domesday Book*, which notes that the coastal area of 3360 acres (from Pevensey to Firle) was under the control of Roger the Cleric. It was home to 68 villeins (a serf tied to the land), 28 plough hands and six labourers (possibly slaves). The area produced salt, had a mill, and one wooden church (possibly the original St Marys in Westham next to Pevensey Castle built by the invading Normans in 1085).

My wife's family (the Reeds) were first mentioned in local parish records back in 1296 (they may have been here much longer, perhaps some of the villeins mentioned in 1086). They are part of the very structure and fabric of our area. Out of the five local names from 1296 records, the Tutts, Erridges, Bodles, Reeds, and Bartholomews, we still know and work with four of the five families. Eastbourne has changed beyond all recognition, but through this land still run these ancient bloodlines.

Chris Erridge, presently 74, (and still cutting my hair from the best barbers shop in town in Susan's Road) will smile knowing what is to follow. As well as fishermen, his family ran pleasure boats along Royal Parade. They also had bathing huts in the summer for tourists (until the council took over in 1920). The bathing huts were often lowered to the water line by ropes and pulleys attached to harnessed horses. Women could sedately step down into the sea in modesty, then return to their hut to be drawn back in as they changed. You can still sometimes spot the iron rings where the ropes went through, along the promenade wall.

The Langham Hotel have one of the original bathing huts, painted in traditional seaside red and yellow. In the summer they put it on show outside their premises, on the corner of Cambridge Road. Royal Parade has changed course slightly, much like a river, as more beach was reclaimed and properties built. It explains the strange route and numbering of the houses around Treasure Island (that drives new postmen crazy).

Here is Ted Hide and myself holding up two of the best books on the old Eastbourne Families, The Pleasure Boatmen of Eastbourne and The Fishermen of Eastbourne, both written by Ted in 2007 and in 2009. Ted has been invaluable with his resources and information.

Here are Chris's Dad, George Henry Erridge, and Granddad George John 'Quack' Erridge, one of Eastbourne's oldest fishing families. Nearly all the local fishermen had nicknames as you will find out. Both of them went across on the MV Amasis to help with the evacuation of Dunkirk in June 1940, (Operation 'Cycle').

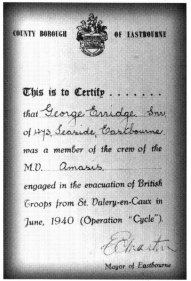

George John Erridge's certificate awarded for his part in Operation Cycle from the Mayor of Eastbourne.

We are going to begin our story with our walk at the far end of town. By starting at the old fishing hamlet at Holywell Flats, and the need for the town to use the water below them, I can cover the growth of Eastbourne and still make the book an easy flowing read.

Holywell, pronounced 'holly' (like Christmas holly) by some locals, is the area that sits beneath the Sugar Loaf on the last tip of Eastbourne's promenade. It is where our town reverts from its prim and proper seaside elegance back to wild Mother Nature. It is where the cliffs meet the sea. It is where

Eastbourne stops and our story starts.

To many it is just another beauty spot, but if you scratch the surface a whole pool of wonderful history bubbles up, including a blessed 'Holy Well'.

For a huge period in human history Holywell was incredibly important, but by the Second World War it had faded and much of its early life forgotten. I have put in plenty of pictures along the way to show you how in a short period, not only Holywell changed, but everything around it as well.

I have to briefly explain why Holywell is so special to me. Special enough to trigger the writing of a book. We all have priceless early memories; you know, those golden memories of youth wrapped in hazy sunshine and spread with a good dollop of nostalgia. As a child I would play in the rock pools at Holywell, prawning, shrimping and catching the tiny fish that scurried around the pools, trapped by the outgoing tide. Years later, as a fearless teenager I would make my way to the dangerous but exhilarating Holywell Reef. There I would fish in the breaking surf for wild Spring Bass.

As a keen-eyed and excited youngster I learnt from the old masters, the retired fishermen who were scattered along the shore like the pebbles they once dragged their boats over. They sat in the sun staring towards the horizon and just like they once cast their old nets, they would spin their tales to any eager ear that passed. There was Ken Warner, John Ball, Frank Scutt and many more. They took me, their keen student, under their wings, off to their secret places to hunt the elusive eater crabs and seek out the precious lobsters hidden beneath the seaweed strewn rocks. Over the years I watched and learned as I saved my shillings. One day I turned up with some stainless steel French gin nets for prawning. Oh, how they laughed when I turned up with my shiny new implements. They looked so hard and bright compared to their soft hand-sewn nets; that was until I pulled up 46 huge prawns in one scoop. From then on the masters knew I had studied their skills well.

There's nothing quite like fresh prawns boiled in salt water and seaweed (with a bay leaf for flavour). This 'catch of the sea' is hard, enjoyable, work. Drizzled with lemon and eaten with a slice of bread 'n' butter they tastes like heaven. Prawns (or shrimp to our American friends) take on the colour of the sea. If the water is clear they turn translucent but if the water is sandy they become perfectly camouflaged. Once cooked they turn pink.

I can still see John Ball in my mind's eye, leaning on his ten foot bamboo prawning pole, smoking a roll-up from his pouch of Golden Virginia. At his feet the corks from his gin nets bobbed in the deep gullies under the shadow of the Beachy Head Lighthouse. He timed each lift of his nets with each cigarette smoked until he had enough prawns for the family. As we walked back along the lonely cliff paths late at night, out would come the tales that only old fisher folk can tell, of ghosts and murder, smuggling and war, all mixed with humour. I can still see the smoke from John's ciggy, trailing into the moonlight as he puffed along, his nets thrown over one shoulder, his full prawn bag over the other. As we strode into the darkness his prawn pole would clip the chalk and I imagined a one-legged pirate straight out of a scene from Treasure Island. He could have been striding up to the Admiral Benbow Inn to meet his drunken shipmates.

Here is Frank Scutt in action, one of the finest rock-men I have ever known (as well as an amazing footballer and cricketer). Frank is on the outer reef at Holywell with his gin nets and pole. He is hunting for prawns and lobster. This can be a dangerous place for those with little experience of the fast tides. Frank was still prawning in his 80's.

Then there was Frank, who would show me his secret lobster spots where the monsters lived. While we hunted he told tales, such as the little Irishman who popped out of nowhere one misty evening. He chatted to Frank at his favourite spot, 'The Gong', on the edge of the wilderness where only the wild things grow. One moment they were gossiping away and the next, the little man vanished. With miles of open sea, sand and rocks, there was no explanation except a ghostly one. Frank had grown up in the war years and spilled tales of Messerschmitt attacks and ack-ack fire, of shipwrecks and bombings. When we prawned, his memories poured out over the rock pools and together we would relive the long lost days of his youth.

Eastbourne is full of ghostly goings on. One of the most famous was the ghost of Molly Downing. Molly ran a sweetshop just off the seafront, along from where Fusciardi's Café is today. She made a small income from making boiled sweets and selling them to sailors, fishermen and tourists along the seafront. It was only after she died in 1864 that her name became known by everyone in the town. Mr Cook, the man who had purchased her home, told the papers that sometime after midnight he was awoken with a start. Through the moonlight he could clearly see someone standing next to his bed. He immediately recognised the deceased Molly. He called to her but she disappeared through the wall towards the seafront. Later that morning her old neighbours, the Hide family, were preparing their boats on the beach for their fishing trip when they saw her watching them, a white light emanating around her. James Hide knew Molly well as he had lived next to her little sweet shop. James and his sons stood frozen to the spot, but when he summoned up the courage to move towards her and call her name, she burst into flames and disappeared. Understandably James Hide and his sons decided to go straight home. They took it as an omen not to go to sea that day and that Molly was warning them of danger. Later that afternoon a huge squall erupted at sea in the area the Hides were going to fish. It could have easily upturned their boat.

Molly's little sweet shop has long gone where she boiled up sweets for the tourists and fishermen. It was where the iron railings and seat are now, next to Ye Old Bakery and the Hide's home at No37. But has Molly gone!

Ken Warner would make me laugh so hard I would almost choke as I worked with him selling fish at his Beach Road fish shop on Saturday mornings. He would tell such tales that only an idiot would believe them, but what stories they were. I was always sceptical about his mad adventures. That all changed one night when I was sitting by my Tilley lights, fishing at

Langney Point. I was on my own when out of the corner of my eye I caught a movement in the black sea; a figure was striding out of the darkness like Neptune, a huge trident over his shoulder. As he moved through the sea mist I could hear my name being called. I nearly wet myself and died on the spot. Pinned to my seat in absolute terror with my jaw low enough to scoop shingle, I eventually recognised the familiar shape of Ken, his deep laugh rolling in with the surf. He was dragging a seine net along the dark shoreline, hoping for a Dover Sole or two. The trident turned out to be no more than the thick rope pulling his net. From then on I believed a few more of his crazy tales. God, those were magical days.

CHAPTER 2

"DON'T GO EAST OF THE PIER MY DEAR, DON'T GO EAST OF THE PIER."

If, after reading this book you feel inspired to actually do this walk, you will need to get to Meads, which to some ageing residents, is still fondly known as the Belgravia of Eastbourne. Meads High Street was once an individual area, separated from the town by sweeping cornfields. The superb, mainly Victorian properties were built on a flat plateau at the foot of the South Downs. On early maps it is sometimes referred to as Medsey.

Meads, with its unique selection of high class shops, old banks and even older customers, was the 'posh' end of town. It now blends seamlessly into Eastbourne. I once met a snobby old dear who instructed me that when you come to Eastbourne you never walk eastward past the pier. That is where the un-desirables reside! Including the cockle sellers. She also said that any person of quality knows about the invisible class line that divides Eastbourne. "If you were buying property you should stand with your back to the pier and only buy property to the left." Luckily, much (but not all) of that old snobbery has disappeared.

From Meads High Street make your way along the wiggly road

up towards my old school, St Bede's (now just 'Bede's'). The road turns into Holywell Road, which leads up past the curving brickwork of the Pilot Inn to the top end of the seafront. The Pilot was once the haunt of the local Holywell fishermen and for a time was run by the Hide family, one of Eastbourne's oldest fishing families.

St Bede's is where I spent my time as a boarder, mixing with pupils from all over the planet; Bano the African prince with a smile that dazzled everyone and a voice as loud as a foghorn. Paul Vogel the stroppy American lad who was going to become president, and many more young characters, most with one thing in common; we were kids away from our families at boarding school.

We were a happy band of brothers as we learned, fought and played together, absorbing information from our enthusiastic teachers as we went. Sure, I felt the searing pain from a polished slipper a few times. The end of that type of school doctrine was still years away. Once I even took the brunt of a chalkboard rubber travelling at the speed of light, although it was by accident! It was hurled through space by our maths teacher Mr Bagnall, who was a mean fast bowler on the cricket pitch. Bagnall was a small wiry man; if he had an ounce of fat on him it was well hidden. He seemed to live on his nerves but he was a superb teacher and to us no less than a genius. He would explain unexplainable things as his mind poured out onto the blackboard in squeals of high pitched chalk. He was normally a sure shot, seldom missing his mark with the chalk. However this time he was hurling the heavier weight of the rubber. He missed his intended mark completely. It was meant for Roland Neville who was sitting next to me. We were at the back of the class and Roland was sniggering to himself while quietly reading *The Beano*, which he had folded between the pages of his homework book. After I came to my senses my worried teacher gave me two precious team points, as hush money of course. They were the easiest points I had ever earned, and as an added bonus I had a nice red lump on my conk to boast about. All in all St Bede's was a brilliant school with great teachers, and each new intern soon felt at home in their latest surroundings.

The dorms were a unique experience. After dinner, homework, and baths, regularly patrolled by the ever vigilant, rotund, and very matronly matron, we went to our different dormitories. St Bede's when I was there was almost entirely a boy's school, very different from today. In the dorms we would chat, read letters from home, play cards or games and finish projects. After an hour or so 'lights out' would be shouted or sometimes a teacher would come and turn them off. In the dark we would quietly chat, and if we were too noisy a teacher would shout up the stairs for us to 'keep it down'. Some of our discussions were about the different countries that many of the pupils came from, or what our fathers did.

One discussion sticks in my mind as clear as day: are you gay? Tricky question for an adolescent; how would we know? One of the lads came up with a crazy solution. He was a lightly built American who used Pearl Drops on his teeth to make them shine. He had a well-stocked, and even better locked tuck box, full of strange delights, like peanut butter'n'jello and rainbow coloured bubble gum. Occasionally he would hand out some of his treasure. "It's easy ain't it," he drawled in the dark. "You Brits 'ave to understand what makes us boys tick. Now, I have a sure-fired way to tell if you's gay or not. The only broad that works 'ere, besides Missus Pyemont is Matron, right? So if you don't fancy Matron, you must be gay! Simple, eh?" There was a deafening silence as to our utter dismay we all pulled up mental images of our chubby, middle-aged matron. One of the lads piped up with a little forced enthusiasm, "Well…She has nice eyes!" A low groan erupted from another bed as it became clear that its occupant clearly didn't fancy her.

Then the laughter started, a few giggles at first, then more and more as we all realised how stupid the idea was. In the end the whole dorm erupted into uncontrollable laughter. Suddenly the door flew open and the lights flashed on. "What the hell is going on up here?" We all looked at Mr Cousins, our teacher, while rubbing our eyes and sniggering. "Well sir," I said cheekily, "we think we might all be gay! You see we don't fancy Matron." There was a long pause, then a little snort from our teacher. "For God's sake, don't be so daft. Now shut up the lot of you or there will be points deducted in the morning." The lights went out and the door slammed. We could hear him walking down the creaky wooden steps mumbling to himself, "Have you ever heard anything so ludicrous, not fancying Matron…, gay?" As his footsteps drifted away we could hear him laughing and we all fell asleep with smiles on our faces. The next day Matron could not understand the strange looks. Even after strenuous interrogation not one of us cracked and told her what had happened the night before.

Before my stay at St Bede's I had never slept by the sea before.

I found out that there is a huge difference because of the light reflecting off the water. As dawn broke I'd watch the sun creep over the horizon and throw giant shadows over our dormitory ceilings. While the other boys slept I would quietly slip out of bed. In my new pyjamas I would tiptoe along the wooden floor to the high sash windows and there I would see a sight made in heaven. In the early mornings you could sometimes see the west wind, warmed by the first rays of the sun, coming across a golden sea. It would ruffle the flat water as it moved closer and closer towards the shore. Occasionally, on gentle days, as the tide fell away, a low sea mist would coat the blue shining bay. The outer ridge of Holywell Reef would rise from the sea, like some giant weed-covered serpent. It seemed like it was cutting its way across the sweeping bay towards Hastings, far off in the shimmering distance. To an imaginative boy it was a wild place full of mystery and magic.

On the horizon, when weather permitted, there was usually a cluster of ships around a shallow sandbank, about seven miles out. It used to be called Wide Mouth Shoal but after the ship HMS Royal Sovereign ran aground it became known as The Royal Sovereign Shoal, with a lightship permanently anchored there to warn other passing vessels. They were busily building an amazing structure to replace the old Sovereign Lightship, which had bobbed on the bouncy sea for many years. It would warn passing sailors of the deadly rocks, shoals, and sandbanks nearby with three flashes every 15 seconds. Christiani & Nielsen (a Danish company at the time) was doing what seemed impossible, building a lighthouse on water! They were paid over £2,000,000 by Trinity House to achieve this momentous task. It was completed in 1971. The Sovereign Light Tower still stands there to this day. However, to my massive disappointment as a child, it only flashed once every 19 seconds. In 2019 Trinity House decided to decommission the Royal Sovereign and work is scheduled to begin in 2020 to remove it from the seabed. I'll miss it.

It is hard to imagine today but in the 1830's, as this sketch by Mary Thomas shows, Meads was little more than a few farm buildings and houses nestling at the foot of the South Downs.

The stunning Cornfield Terrace gets its name from the cornfields it was built over. The building (now in town) has hardly changed.

These two pictures of the Pilot Inn in Meads shows how, although the property has changed since the first picture was taken in 1885, the area today still holds clues to its past.

At Holywell the last ancient water still pours from the cliff face and is crystal clear. After rough weather shingle can often obscure the well. However you can always see the fresh water running down the beach at low tide. Look carefully at the cup it is full.

The steps to the beach at Holywell are steep and dangerous so take care. Notice the Sugar Loaf peeking out at the top. Did it once have a light at night? Why else would there be a path to the top of it? There used to be no need for steps to the beach at Holywell as the chalk gently dropped down to the sea, allowing easy access for the fishermen and their boats. Looking down from the steps to the beach you can still see lots of the debris left behind from the thriving chalk quarry and fishing hamlet.

CHAPTER 3
THE SUGAR LOAF

From Bede's we carry on with our walk down the path between the school and St Helen's Gardens, where the old Holywell Inn once stood. It fed and watered weary travellers coming off the high hill paths of the South Downs. Our circular track leads firstly to the Sugar Loaf (Pinnacle Point), then down to the beach, along to Holywell, and then back up to the main road and Bede's.

When I was a kid I was a terrible street urchin, escaping from school and home alike. I would cycle around Eastbourne for hours. That was probably the reason that my parents forked out the extortionate sum of £85 a term for my confinement at boarding school in the first place. Why am I telling you this? Because it was on these endless outings that I often bumped into the most interesting local Eastbourne characters.

There was an old fisherman who used to sit in the sun at St Helen's Gardens. He told me that he well remembered the noise from the countless steel-rimmed wagon wheels and open carts. They would roll down the Holywell Road (the track that survives now was once a well-used road) to fill their barrels full of special 'healing waters'. When Eastbourne became a 'royal watering hole', horse and carts, wagons and trolleys would all return to their various establishments and hotels with the 'healing waters' for their guests, all from Holywell. The tanks of the Eastbourne Waterworks carts held 250 gallons each. Even today you can often see people fetching the precious water from the last spring at the base of the white cliffs below the Sugar Loaf.

When you make your way down the path and turn the first bend you are confronted by the impressive Sugar Loaf, jutting upwards like a church spire, framing one of the most beautiful and dramatic coastlines in the world. It can be dangerous near the cliff edge, so be careful and stick to the paths.

No one today is absolutely sure why the Sugar Loaf was originally cut out where it is, but I have a theory. Even today, all overgrown, it is imposing. It is shaped into a rough point that was obviously hacked out of the chalk with some great effort. Now it is quite blunt, broken away by tourists and time, but when I was a kid it was more conical shaped and had paths around both sides of it.

The reason this outcrop was called the 'Sugar Loaf' or 'Sugar Lump', is that it resembled the early large blocks of 'pyramid shaped' sugar lumps supplied to the shops. When customers called to buy sugar from their local grocers, the shopkeeper would simply chip off what was required. In recent years it has been renamed Pinnacle Point and when I was a kid it was also called Gibraltar Rock.

My theory is simple. If you wanted to let others know where

fresh drinking water was (not salted, stagnant or polluted pond water) how would you do that? A sign, a big sign, that could be seen from sea or shore from miles away. If you walk down to the sea, away from the cliff face and look back up to the Sugar Loaf, you can see what a superb monument it is. It is also directly above the fresh water flowing from the cliff face. It is a well-known fact that many early travellers used the sea as an easier method of moving around the country. A pointer to fresh water would be a real bonus.

There may also be a religious significance. The most important times in all religious calendars are guided by the Earth and the Sun. Two of the significant dates of the year are the mid-summer and mid-winter solstices. Years ago I had dropped my wife Yana off at work and was having a brisk walk, out of a bitterly cold North wind with Rolly, my dearly missed little Patterdale. It was in bleak midwinter, the shortest day of the year. Holywell was perfect as I was protected by the cliffs. While walking up by the Sugar Loaf I stopped to catch my breath and I noticed the sun start to come over the horizon. I climbed up the small path behind the tip of the Sugar Loaf, dragging Rolly reluctantly behind me; the steep narrow path comes up close to the back of the highest point of the Sugar Loaf. To my amazement the sun popped up out of the sea, directly in line with the point where I was standing. It was one of those deeply inspiring moments. It showed that the Sugar Loaf is in perfect alignment with the Winter Solstice. Is that just luck? I doubt it. It is the only day of the year that the sun hits that exact spot. I believe the path and the point of the Sugar Loaf were ancient markers for the well and it was made precisely to mark the shortest day of the year.

As I am writing I must add one word of caution, the area of beach below the Sugar Loaf is currently a centre for well-aged and well-rounded nudists in the summer, which shocks some (just some) of our old Eastbourne dears!

There is a tale that the Sugar Loaf may have also been a marker for the fishermen to find their way back through the barrier of rocks on the outer reef. Many years ago a channel was blasted out of the reef so that the fishermen could safely get through to the beach on a falling tide. Coincidence or not, the Sugar Loaf is the perfect marker for the gap and the water pouring from the cliff face.

In our modern world, we take fresh water for granted, but it is our most basic and fundamental need. Without drinking water we would all die very quickly. Just look at how many adverts still appear regularly on our televisions asking for donations to provide this most rudimentary need to people less fortunate than ourselves. Fresh water was probably the main reason that the first settlements existed at this spot.

Later on in our history, as Christianity came to our shores, with seafaring priests and monks, it is easy to imagine them setting up shop right here, using the Sugar Loaf as a marker for the fresh water. Then they could preach, spread Christianity, and dish out water in equal amounts. It sounds far-fetched today, but all around Britain and the world that is exactly what happened.

Interestingly, as I was writing part of this story in May of 2015, a water main burst near Hailsham. Within a day bottled water sold out everywhere in the area. As water trucks brought fresh drinking water the following day, fights broke out in the car parks. All that was just after one day without water!

Some of the evidence of our early roots in Eastbourne is now in the British Museum in London. Discoveries over the years have brought to light our Neolithic, Stone Age, Bronze Age, Iron Age, Roman, (the Roman town of Anderida is under some of Eastbourne) heritage and much more. The National Trust have recently been excavating near their café at Birling Gap, looking for evidence of the Beaker People (named after their pottery storage jars). They settled here over 4,500 years ago. All of these discoveries are based around sources of fresh water.

We see Eastbourne as a modern town but in reality it sits on earth used by our ancestors for millennia. The first evidence of humans living here (in what we now call Britain) stretches back between ice ages and time. A flint hand-axe, found just up the road at East Dean, was astonishingly dated to over 500,000BC. In fact Bede's sits on earthworks left by our Iron Age cousins who lived there a mere 2,500 years ago. Why at Holywell? Because even in the driest summers they had fresh water pouring from the cliffs.

One of the most fascinating characters who collected artefacts from our ancestors was the Shepherd of Beachy Head, Stephen Blackmore. The old shepherd died in 1919 and is buried in Seaford Cemetery. While Stephen tended his flock he kept a sharp eye out for 'worked flint'. Over his many years on the South Downs he accumulated nearly 900 Neolithic flint tools. In 1892 he donated around 700 of them to the Sussex

Archaeological Society. I've been told a few still remain with the Eastbourne Museum Services.

What I am trying to say is that although lots of the area's history has been lost, there is a rich layer of clues, which still allows us to glimpse through a window into the past.

The area that Eastbourne now inhabits must have seemed like a haven for our ancestors. They had food from the hills and sea, fresh water flowing from the chalk, shelter from the cold north winds and abundant wood for building and fuel. From the end of our last Ice Age, the foot of our South Downs was just the most perfect place to live.

It was right here, on the last remains of the plateau above Holywell where our first local recorded ancestors lived, loved and died.

Though a few families stretched along the coast, the original fishermen of our area fell mainly into two camps, the Holywell Fishermen and the other families at an area called The Stade. The Stade was a flat beach area along by the Sea Houses, just eastward of Eastbourne Pier today. The fishing station was between the Sea Houses and Marine Parade, although the fishermen would often use the entire length of the shallow sweeping bay to beach their craft when the weather was inclement. At The Stade wooden groynes were built to protect the shingle beach and capstans placed along the shoreline to allow the boats to be hauled in. Visiting vessels would be charged a berthing fee, but the local fishermen were allowed to use The Stade facilities for free.

Today the last beach fishermen are centred around Bob Page's old fish shop (currently Southern Head Fishing Co) on the beach, between Treasure Island and the Spray Water Sports Centre (currently Active Buzz), along by Fisherman's Green. If you look at a map, the fishermen's beaches stretch roughly between Beach Road and Channel View Road at Princes Park (once the beginning of The Crumbles). They still have their rights to beach access there.

The heavier boats are now berthed at Sovereign Harbour, which was built over the last remains of The Crumbles to the east. The Crumbles being a large lump of waste land (actually once called The Waste). All that was there when I was a kid, besides the Martello Towers, was a few boats, a gravel works, a rifle range and some wonderful semi-saline lakes where perch thrived in numbers to satisfy my limited poaching skills.

The Sugar Loaf in 2016 with Max the Dalmatian

The Sugar Loaf has many names including Pinnacle Point and Gibraltar Point. Shown here in 1990, it was much more open back then.

This hugely important sketch of Holywell House was made in 1873 by one of the Garland family whilst holidaying in Eastbourne. It is one of the few images of the house that sat opposite where Bede's is today. Originally it was an inn built by the Hart family and later owned by the Coppard family. The National Archives show that it passed to Samuel Coppard in 1880 who passed it onto John Hide in 1889. John Hide owned the Pilot Inn at the time. The house is where Ted Hide's grandfather was born. It was demolished around the same time as the Holywell Hamlet was destroyed in the 1890's. The path in the sketch ran down to the fishermen's dwellings at Holywell Flats and the chalk quarry.

It is difficult to imagine Eastbourne promenade before construction began. It was little more than a few cottages strung between the Martello Towers and Redoubt Fortress, the rise was known as Mount Pleasant. A beautiful wild area that the Duke would tame, building in in its place one of the most impressive Victorian promenades in the World.

The View we see today has changed little since the late 19th Century. It grew quickly, with amazing Victorian engineering reshaping the low cliff edges and replacing them with a tiered promenade. The new fortifications protected the hotels and allowed easy access to the beaches, including all the benefits the new tourist trade was after. It was a Victorian master-piece that tamed Mother Nature and allowed the massive construction of the hotels. The Carpet Gardens are unique to Eastbourne and beautifully maintained.

The Martello Towers get their name from the original Tower of Mortella at Mortella Point in Corsica. They predate Eastbourne, being built between 1804 and 1812. 103 forts were built along the South Coast moving eastward from Seaford to Suffolk. They were built in response to Napoleon's plans to invade England but were never used in action. 'Nasty little Napoleon' at 5ft 9" tall was actually above average height for the period but British propaganda painted him as a 'little upstart' destroying Europe.

Napoleon had gathered an army of 200,000 men to attack England. However a series of setbacks and defeats meant he had to use his troops elsewhere and the attack never materialised. The forts were manned by around 20 men; they are roughly 40 feet high. They are immensely thick (around 8 feet at their thinnest point). On their roof was a cannon that could be spun around 360 degrees to cover all points. The cannon were capable of firing to the next tower along so that each fort could cover an invasion. They were supplied with men and ammunition from three major forts known as Redoubt Fortresses in Harwich, Dymchurch and Eastbourne.

This is the Redoubt Fortress in Eastbourne, started in 1805. In its heyday (around 1812) it would have been home to about 200 men. A ship passed within range of its guns that year but they missed! It was reported that it was a French naval vessel but that was never confirmed. It was the only time in its long history that the gun was fired in anger. The redoubt was in use in some small way right up to WW2. When I was a kid it went through several guises as a wonderful miniature village, a great aquarium and several cafés. It is currently a military museum open in the summer months. Although many Martello Towers have been destroyed or swallowed up by modern building the Eastbourne Redoubt still holds commanding views of the sea at Splash Point.

Chapter 4
Holly or Holy?

Before we discover whether it is 'holy' or 'holly' we first need to find out exactly where Holywell originally was!

Holywell today is considered by most to be the area where the Dotto Train stops, by the Holywell Tea Chalet and bathing huts, at the far western end of the promenade. Some call it Holywell Retreat or Holywell Beach. However the original Holywell is at the end of Holywell Road which ran down besides Bede's School. It finishes at Holywell Pumping Station. You'll not be able to see that as it is now a restricted area.

Holywell Pumping Station is where the Holywell Fishing Hamlet was. The hamlet predates 'new' Eastbourne. The first recorded fishing station was certainly established firmly at Holywell Hollow and Holywell Flats by 1785. The area where the fishermen's sheds were established was also known as Collin's Flats. It is from this period onward that information about the dwellings and inhabitants of the Holywell hamlet becomes more fact than fiction. However, there is little doubt fishermen and their families would have been using that area for centuries before that.

Before we get going we must also address some mis-conceptions about the pronunciation of Holywell.

Although Holywell is spelt with one 'l' some locals still pronounce it like the holly bush with two 'll's'. For as long as anyone can remember, locals have always called the place Hollywell, everyone else, holidaymakers, visitors, and new-comers pronounce it as it is spelt, Holywell. This has caused a lot of problems with writers, historians, and even map makers. So what's it all about?

A few people say that the original name Holywell came from where chalk was cut from the cliffs, (some of which was used for the winding road to Beachy Head) and that Holywell was an abbreviation of the words 'hollow place'. Most of the chalk actually came from Gore Chalk Pit round the corner, and at a much later date. That area survives today as The Italian Gardens (we will be going by there later in the story).

I can see a few people calling a chalk pit a 'hollow place' but a chalk pit was a chalk pit, so that doesn't hold much water.

Some even say that a holly tree once grew there, and the name went from holly tree to Holywell. If that was the case, with wild holly trees being so abundant, every other place in the country would be called the same!

To confuse matters more, there were countless other local names, Holywell Hollow, Holywell Flats, Holywell Retreat, Holywell Ledge, Holywell House, Holywell Hamlet, and Holywell Bank. These were all old names used for roughly the same area and spelt with a single 'l'. Now, out of all the early maps I found, there was just one 18th Century map using the name Hollywell, another mentions Holly Well Furlong.

Interestingly it is from about the same time that written documentation starts to appear about the Holy Well at Holy-well. In John Royer's book of 1787 he makes a specific mention of the spring at Holy Well having healing powers. Holy Well rose to prominence once again under the 'new town' of Eastbourne, where 'purifying waters' were a big draw. Much more of that later as we build a town.

This fascinating ancient lay or poem that was discovered and reprinted in the local paper in 1862. Due to the poor image and old spelling I am not sure if I have all the wording exact.

HOLYWELL

Drink to me from this cup,
And I will pledge with mine;
Holywell's sweet water sup,
No need to want for wine.

I've supt on ale and on stout,
No honour 'twas to me,
Now I imbibe the waters clear,
That trickle near the sea.

To family, beer money send,
And let thy good deeds shine.
The crystal stream libatious friend,
Is purer far than wine.

Then fill from Holywell thy cup,
From thence too I'll fill mine;
The rill that filters through the rock,
Is sweeter far than wine.

Somewhere in Meads, locals say that there was once a chapel that was dedicated to our own 'holy well'. Rumours persist that the chapel was near the foot of Warren Hill and The Duke's Drive (now Upper Duke's Drive) but some say it's under South Cliff Towers! It was dedicated to St Gregory, who was the first Pope to try and convert the pagan Anglo Saxons to Christianity. Apparently it fell into disrepair after a French raiding party from Dieppe destroyed much of it while stealing its bells. There are supposed to be some remains of the ruins. However Meads has encroached on, and been built around so many old structures, I have never located it.

Interestingly in the summer of 2010 the last remains of Holywell, down on the beach where the water still flows, was blessed in a large religious ceremony with two priests and several sermons. It was followed by singing and ceremonial drinking of the water. I think there is still a YouTube clip on it.

To finish off. I know this is going to ruffle a few local feathers but to my mind there is only one dependable and logical reason that Holywell is named Holywell. Like so many special places around the world it is almost definitely because Holywell has the amazing gift of pure water that pours forth from the cliff face, day and night, 365 days a year.

It was this water that would be needed to quench the thirst of a new town. Little did the inhabitants at Holywell know, they had a huge fight coming!

This is the Gore Chalk Pit circa 1919. The Holywell area was slowly turning from a working chalk pit into a tourist attraction before being completely laid out into formal gardens in 1922.

CHAPTER 5
WELLS AND WISHES

For 'new' Eastbourne to exist as a thriving town, water was the first and most essential ingredient. By the 19th Century spa towns were popping up all over the country. The search for healthy drinking water was reaching a frenzy.

Let's look at a few towns around the country and their relationship with clean water. It is a fascinating insight into our evolution. The waters of Malvern for instance, attracted the rich and famous from Princess Victoria to Charles Darwin. The town consequently boomed.

As the railways spread across Britain the famed healing quality of water, from Bath to Harrogate, Leamington to Tunbridge Wells were suddenly, and for the first time in human history, within easy travelling distance for the masses. Loads of wealthy tourists meant loads of money to be made. The trains brought in well-heeled visitors by the thousands who would 'take the cure'. Healing 'miracle' waters, those elixirs of life were good for everything from gout to spasms and fortunes were being made. Of course treasuring water is nothing new. Perhaps the most famous watering hole in England is Bath.

When the Romans first heard about a magical well, that poured warm water from inside the earth, they put it down to local superstition. However, when they came across the wells, which really were pouring out more than a million litres of steaming green water a day (even in the middle of Winter), they soon realised they had discovered something more valuable than gold. By 70 AD, as they had unified Europe under one rule, one currency, and one law, they had built one of the most impressive towns in the Roman Empire. They cleverly dedicated the temple to the local Celtic deity, Sulis, and Minerva, their own Goddess of War and Wisdom. Aquae Sulis Minerva became one of the most visited and luxurious sites in Roman Britain, with underfloor heating, steam baths, rest rooms, massage parlours, pools, and saunas. A retired Roman dignitary could gossip with an off duty soldier, or flirt with a local Celt all while buying snacks and soaking in the healing waters. Under Roman rule, with the free movement of people throughout Europe, Aquae Sulis Minerva became one of its most popular centres of luxury.

When the Georgians reinvented Bath, 1,300 years after the Romans had left, it became the social centre of England, and the winter watering place for wealthy Londoners. All once again, centred around its water (disgusting as it is to drink). Before the Georgian rebirth, with its wonderful honey stone buildings, Bath still held its image for possessing magical healing water. Mary of Modena, the second wife of James II, was desperate for a male heir to settle a fractious England. Late in 1687 she very noisily travelled to Bath and took the 'wonder waters'. No sooner had she done so she fell pregnant and on 10 June 1688 she produced a male heir for King James. This miracle, meant to calm the country, was short-lived. Some said it was a little too convenient to produce an heir to order! Rumours abounded that the child was a 'changeling'. Some even say it was smuggled into the birthing chamber in a bedpan! Whatever the real truth, it never helped matters as later that year the King threw the royal seal into the River Thames and ran for France, leaving the throne open for his son-in-law and nephew, William of Orange.

Another well with an even more fascinating story is nearby at Glastonbury. It also dates from a similar period. Christian mythology tells that the Chalice Well, or the Red Spring at the foot of Glastonbury Tor, runs red with the rust from the nails from the Cross of Jesus. The tale goes that Joseph of Arimathea hid the Holy Grail under the well (the Holy Grail being the chalice or vessel from the last Supper that caught drops of blood from Jesus on the cross). From the second he hid the Holy Grail the waters turned red. Apparently it is the iron content in the rocks that gives the water its red tint. Don't you love these ancient tales and legends! You can see how our country and its history is so entwined with water.

All around the country 'holy wells' exist. One of the larger towns in Wales is even called Holywell after its protected well. St Winefride's Well in Flintshire has a wonderful tale of a local beauty having her head reattached after a lord went on the rampage and beheaded her. Whatever the real tale, her shrine and the healing waters have been visited by sick children and believers for centuries. Even Richard the Lion-Heart popped in for a sip. Today, minor miracles occur there on a regular basis.

The tiny cathedral city of Wells in Somerset, just below Bath, has three natural springs bubbling up out of the ground. These were so exceptional that the Bishop of Wells had them walled up and his palace built around them so that the water could be guarded. The man was all heart. As a minor compensation, he had channels cut into the streets so that excess water could run into the High Street. It still does.

Hardly two miles away as the crow flies from Wells is Wookey Hole and the oldest of our sacred waters. My favourite legend when I visited was that King Arthur killed the witch that watched over the well, allowing the poor villagers to drink from it. In truth we know that the earliest recorded human bones in the country have been found there, some apparently dating back a staggering 50,000 years. It seems that not only water pours out from these sources but wonderful tales as well!

Special healing wells, sacred wells and baptismal wells are often called Chalybeate wells, those with health-giving properties. There are still many dotted around Britain. There is no scientific proof (as yet) that the waters do 'miraculously heal' but, as we know, faith has its own power that no one really understands. Subconsciously we still make offerings to water; just look at all the coins in fountains and wells all over the world from Las Vegas to Rome.

My favourite well is St Keyne's Wishing Well, between Liskeard and Looe, down in the West Country. It is a tiny place; so small that even the train is a request stop. If you don't put your hand out it goes straight by. From the station you take a short walk up a narrow lane and you come upon the well of

Saint Keyne, the daughter of an ancient king. There is a great tale that if you go there on your wedding day and make a wish it could be of benefit to you: "Whosoever drinketh the water first, be it man or wife, will be master of the family for life."

Today multi-million pound industries still flourish selling bottled natural mineral water to the public. Tesco's sell Perthshire Natural Water drawn from volcanic rock deep underground, the same water that centuries earlier the locals had found to be pure. Everyone knew even back then that bad water killed!

Here I lie with my two daughters
Died through drinking Cheltenham waters.
Had I stuck to Epsom Salts,
We wouldn't be beneath these vaults!

The Dukes of Devonshire had spent small fortunes building spa towns like Buxton, famous from the time when Mary Queen of Scots had made her pilgrimage there to drink from the miracle waters of St Ann's Well, which they say fell as rainwater thousands of years earlier before bubbling up to the surface.

Talking of Mary Queen of Scots, Scotland has loads of wells and just as many legends surrounding them. They are often referred to as Clootie Wells. St Mary's Well, for example, near the Culloden Battlefield, is decorated with countless strips of cloth or 'Clooties'. The colourful strips blowing in the breeze represent the prayers and wishes of visitors who have made the journey to see the sacred well.

In 1788 King George III had his first major bilious attack. He was advised by the experts of the day to make the arduous journey to Cheltenham to visit a magical well, found on farmland the previous century. Locals believed that the pungent soapy slime would cure everything as long as you drunk a pint of it each morning before breakfast! They do not record if 'mad' King George was cured.

Cheltenham was really the first 'modern' spa town. By 1818, at its Georgian peak, the Pitville Pump Rooms were crowded daily in the 'season', which ran from June to October each year. Entrepreneur, Henry Thompson, had laid in pumps and pumped water from the well to his special bottling factory. Then he sold bottles of slimy water to the crowding tourists to take home. Even the ageing Duke of Wellington was impressed when in 1827 he took water and baths in Cheltenham to ease his aching bones.

As businessmen saw the amazing potential in health resorts, a hundred more spa towns would soon follow.

Derbyshire and The Peak District have the wonderful custom, still going strong today, of 'well dressing'. It is the old pagan ritual that continues to thrive, of decorating the wells with flowers and greenery. Today the practice has been assimilated by the Christian faith and the ceremonies give praise to God for the water, rather than some pagan deity or water spirit.

Our local wishing well in Eastbourne used to be just next to the pier. It was always full of money thrown in by well-wishers! Unfortunately in the 1970's they had to put a steel frame over the wishing well as people had started to steal the money. Sadly, as a sign of the times, it was regularly broken through until the well was removed altogether.

Funnily, up until 2017, the Koi Carp pond at Fishy Business, next to Hilliers Garden Centre (on the Ersham Road to Hailsham) was always layered with coins. Each year for charity, Paul Teague used to pull on his diving gear and fill his buckets up with the offerings he found there.

Even Charles Lutwidge Dodgson, better known to us as Lewis Carol, twisted a holy well into his tales of Alice: *"Once upon a time there were three little sisters,' the dormouse began in a great hurry; 'and their names were Elsie, Lacie, and Tillie; and they lived at the bottom of a well—"*

Dodgson was in fact referring to the Binsey Holy Well of St Margaret, near Oxford. It is where he had taken Alice on one of their afternoon picnics. Binsey Well had been visited by pilgrims since medieval times and was even said to have the power to restore blindness.

It is interesting that long before churches and religious institutions it was the wells that people made their pilgrimages to. Christianity was quick to see the importance of water on local communities. They often built their places of worship close to clean water.

Alban, the first British Martyr was one such case. Around the third century in Verulamium (near where St Albans stands today) Alban gave shelter to a priest running from the Romans.

When the Romans caught up with them he pretended to be the priest (having been quickly converted to Christianity). The priest Amphibalus escaped and when Alban was brought before the magistrate he refused to renounce the priest or his worship of the one true God. For his disobedience he was sentenced to a gruesome death. On a hot June day he was marched up the hill from Verulamium to a place of execution. As he fell to his knees near the top of the hill, a spring burst forth from the ground with pure fresh water. Seeing this miracle the executioner thought the better of chopping off his head so another had to be found. According to the early chronicler The Venerable Bede (which my school was named after), no sooner than Alban had his head removed the executioners eyes popped out! Nasty.

It wasn't long before miracles started happening at the spot and the pilgrimages begun. Now a beautiful cathedral stands near the spot at the top of Holywell Hill. Inside there are shrines to both St Alban and St Amphibalus. Once again water proving its importance.

When the Duke of Devonshire was contemplating the building of his new seaside resort, he would have looked at all the future sources of revenue, and everything else that would attract visitors. Besides his 'pleasure grounds', water, as we shall find out, was the other huge natural resource that he could draw income from.

Even today we are drawn by water and induced to throw things into it. Here is my friend Paul Teague. He is collecting coins thrown into the water of the Koi Carp pond at Fishy Business in June of 2015. Every year, until the business moved, Paul pulled on his wet gear and collected the money for charity.

CHAPTER 6
LEGENDS OF OUR HOLY WELL

Where do the rumours and legends begin of our very own 'holy well'? It has been great fun gathering all the titbits of information. Some led nowhere but others are worth a mention. Luckily for me a few local historians had also been doing some digging. The legends start as early as 1450, when a small community of nuns supposedly looked after the well, handing clean water to weary travellers and locals alike. They would pray for their souls and gain converts as they dished out water and accepted charitable donations of foods and goods.

The nuns possibly disappeared after The Reformation, when many religious houses suffered due to our Tudor monarch. King Henry VIII's zealous money launderings and subsequent wife gatherings changed everything.

There is also a legend based on a little piece of evidence that starts in 1862, when Mother Superior, Harriet Brownlow Byron came to Eastbourne seeking help.

Just down the road from St Bede's is the large and impressive building of All Saints. It is now split into expensive retirement flats but was once a hospital that cared for the sick and dying.

Mother Harriet was instrumental in its construction. Harriet's wealthy family were part of the landed gentry centred around Coulsdon Court in Surrey. Her father was a Member of Parliament and Lord of the Manor of Coulsdon.

Sister Harriet, along with Reverend Upton Richards, established one of the first Anglican Sisterhoods, an order of nuns called the All Saints Sisters of the Poor. They cared for 'aged women,' 'incurables,' and later, orphans. In 1856 Harriet was elected by the High Church Sisterhood as 'Mother for Life' of her order. Her tireless work saw hospitals established, not only in England, but her sisters went around the world with missions. Harriet herself was mentioned many times by Florence Nightingale.

Around 1863, overworked and suffering persistent weakness, Harriet came to Eastbourne to rest and recover. Some tales say that, like so many others, she drank from the 'Holy Waters' of Holywell. Afterwards she found a new lease of life and made an amazing recovery. After returning to London she was very aware of how beneficial Eastbourne had been to her and how it could also help others who were suffering. To repay God, the legend goes that she acquired five acres of prime land from the Duke and oversaw the building of All Saints Hospital, where she used the healing waters for her own patients.

At the time her neighbours were farm workers, fishermen, lime burners and smugglers. Some say that it may have been the impressive building that triggered the planning and expansion of Meads. It is a great story but there is little hard evidence that I can uncover. Except that the hospital and Sister Harriet certainly did exist!

Anyway, the foundation stone of All Saints Convalescent Hospital was laid over cornfields on 19 July 1867, by Fanny Howard, the Duke of Devonshire's sister. The day of celebration was accompanied by services with great feasting and singing. Many of the important dignitaries of the area attended. Over £300 was donated to the hospital and her cause, a staggering amount in 1867. Within two years of energetic building the hospital was ready. Later, as the hospital gained in reputation, a second stage of large building work took place. The foundation stone for All Saints Children's Convalescent Home was laid by the Duchess of Albany and opened by the future king and his wife, the Prince and Princess of Wales, in June of 1891. For over 100 years the dedicated nuns and nurses tended to the sick and dying. The hospital was open to the public every afternoon except Sunday and it was often visited by our Royals who enthusiastically supported All Saints. The hospital closed in 2004.

Times have changed. Now the old building is a selection of plush retirement homes. The breath-taking chapel is still a popular venue. It is currently the only one of its type in the country that holds a license for weddings. In fact it is where my daughter Sarah was married, one misty Spring day in 2015.

The Reverend Mother Harriet Brownlow Byron,
founder of All Saints Sisters of the Poor.

All Saints Convalescent Hospital circa 1869.

All Saints today. The impressive buildings are now flats.

My daughter Sarah on her wedding day to Dominic. The chapel is like a miniature cathedral and stunningly beautiful inside.

Chapter 7

Birth of a Town

When I mentioned earlier that our area has been inhabited for millennia, it really has. One of the most amazing finds was the remains of a skeleton found near Beachy Head in 1953. It turned out (with modern forensic techniques) to be that of a young black woman. She was around 20 and lived on a healthy diet of fish, vegetables and meat. The Beachy Head Lady was from southern Africa and lived during the Roman occupation of Britain. I wonder how she felt about our area? Did she see its beauty while she gathered food and water? She must have seen our land when the great forests of Anderida still swept across them, when wild bear and boar roamed freely. Funny how so many people still think immigration is a modern phenomenon! I have the feeling that as soon as humans developed legs we used them to travel.

Our journey down the old Holywell Road takes you just past the first bend and the fabulous coastal views, as the green downland tumbles to the sea in a dramatic collision of utter beauty. As you get your first look at the Sugar Loaf pointing skyward, like an old church steeple, you are also confronted by huge steel-bolted gates. The signs makes it painfully clear that it's private property.

Extraordinarily, beyond those gates is the winding path that led to one of the original settlements of old Eastbourne. We are going to discover all about it in the coming pages.

It is difficult to imagine today, but there was a much larger plateau of land that dropped gently in flat sections down to the water. There was plenty of room for a settlement on the raised chalk. It was perfectly protected from the ravages of the sea by the protruding cliffs further to the west. In the last hundred years or so, most of the plateau has disappeared, dragged away by the tide. All that remains is a small parcel of land, some of it now protected from the sea by giant granite boulders. They were dropped along the shoreline by our water authority to stop further erosion and protect its water supplies. It is this very land that holds some of the secrets of Eastbourne's early inhabitants. It is also one of the stepping stones that helped to make our town.

The remains of the Beachy Head Lady, who live here around 2,000 years ago, were discovered in 1953. She was African and lived on a rich seafood diet. We can only imagine what her world was like. This amazing image, reconstructed from her skull, was from the Eastbourne Ancestors exhibition that ran at The Pavilion Tea Rooms throughout 2014.

Family legend from two sides of our relatives, the Cottingtons and the Reeds, tell that when the Carpet Gardens were first laid out by the pier, they copied the pattern of the ancient Roman mosaics or tesserae found underneath the base of the fountains. It was possibly the site of a Roman manor as some foundations were also discovered. People think that Eastbourne's seafront is quite new, but the layout of the land from Holywell to the Pier has changed very little over the centuries. One picture shows Jack Reed laying out the formal design for summer. Even when working as foreman, he always wore a suit and tie!

Some of the early Eastbourne Families, including Jack Reed, (fourth from the left). Road building along the seafront was hard and heavy work, even with the invention of the first steam trucks. However, when fishing was poor it was sought-after paid work.

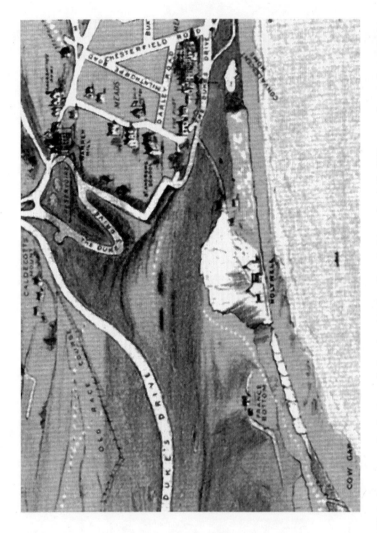

This old 19th Century map clearly shows the hamlet of Holywell tucked into the chalk cliff face on the seashore. The image was taken shortly before the hamlet was seized and closed.

This is only part of the hamlet, painted by Amos Luck, as much of it was tucked around the corner up against the chalk face. It does however give us an idea of what was there.

This image by local artist, Joe Shepherd, shows a clearer image of the steam-operated pumping station (and coal shed in the foreground). It shows that in 1890 the pumping station was working alongside the last of the Holywell Families (before they were finally moved off the land for fear of contamination).

This wonderful painting is by Alfred Erridge, possibly of the Boniface and Collins Cottages at Holywell Flats. Interestingly this type of dwelling had changed little for centuries. Windows were one of the few improvements that came in the 19th Century, replacing the wooden shutters. Alfred made it in 1887 and it is currently owned by his relative, Chris Erridge. You can clearly see how prominent the Sugar Loaf was behind the dwelling before it became so overgrown.

Here is one of the finest images of the Holywell hamlet. It is in the Ted Hide Collection and captures the area in its prime. Within a few short years all this would be destroyed and a way of life for the early fishing families of Eastbourne lost forever. The Collins, Woods and Bonifaces were three of the families that probably lived there.

The beach at Holywell was a hive of activity throughout the 19th Century. It was far shallower with easy access to Holywell Flats and the fishermen's cottages. If you take a look at low tide, you can still see some of the remains on the beach today. Ted Hide Collection.

The coastal path once led straight from Holywell to French's Farm then onward to Beachy Head Farm. All that is left now is the playing fields for Bede's School.

Lobster and crab fishing was a main staple of the Holywell fishermen. The reefs that lay off the coast, all along to Seaford are prime hunting grounds for the valuable crustaceans.

These gates now block the ancient path that led to the Holywell Hamlet.

Chapter 8
The Old Fishing Hamlet of Holywell

All is silent at the gates now, just the birdsong and skylark, often held on a westerly sea breeze. Up until the 1890's there was the busy clamour and bustle of a thriving community at Holywell. Where the gates are today you would have been able to see a whole hamlet laid out before your eyes. You would have seen the Holywell Coastguard Station, manned day and night to keep a keen eye on the area. You would also have seen the fishermen hauling their catches from their boats up the shallow paths to their homes and to the smoking racks. There would have been children playing outside the wooden weatherboard buildings. Nets would be piled up or hanging in the drying sheds; lobster pots, floats and ropes strewn all around. There would have been horses, dogs, chickens, cats, and women lifting water from the wells, watering their seaweed-rich vegetable beds.

Most importantly, the fisher families lived on a chalk outcrop. That chalk had tremendous value. The fisher families would have worked the chalk that surrounded them creating a chalk quarry. Chalk-limestone, and all its constituents was a huge cash crop for the hamlet, often bringing in more money than the fish. Most weeks there would have been men working the chalk pits and lime kilns that were tucked into the hillside at Holywell.

Fortunately for us, just before the community was destroyed, a local sign writer, Amos Luck, took the time to sit down with his easel and brushes to capture the disappearing community. Amos was the son of the proprietor of The Ship Inn in Meads. His painting is one of the only images of the hamlet to survive. It is currently in our impressive Town Hall.

The families of the hamlet lived on all that nature provided. They had an abundance of food from the sea, rabbits and chickens from the downland and anything they could grow. I say chickens because they traded with French's old chicken farm in Whitebred Hollow (which has long since gone). John Ball once told me that both of the farmer's sons went off to war and never came home, so when the old farmer died, Mother Nature slowly reclaimed his farm until no trace survived. Today, Bede's uses some of it for their playing fields. Also, milk and cheese were bartered from Beachy Head farm, in exchange for fish.

Fishing has regular seasons. The local fishermen knew them well. The herring season was October and November. December to January was sprat season. June, July and August were crab & lobster season, some from Horse Rocks (known locally as The Hoss, out near the Sovereign Lighthouse) and the rest all the way along the rocky coast from Holywell to Birling Gap and Cuckmere Haven. During this period the Birling Gap Hotel became the fishermen's local, sometimes camping out for a week or more with their pots. June and July was also mackerel time and the fisherman would chase the fish, 'shooting' their nets in front of the shoals that were moving along the English Channel. The bass and pollock would move into shallower water once the water hit ten degrees Celsius. Then in the colder months the cod and whiting would move down from the cool Scandinavian climes of the North Sea, foraging along the coastline.

When the tides were wrong, or stormy weather prevented the boats going out to sea, the Holywell Men would concentrate on making lime, quicklime and slaked lime, all from the natural materials that surrounded them. As they cut away at the chalk downland they were actually making more level land on which they could retreat as the tides nibbled away at the coastline below them. This constant use of the downland shaped the very landscape on which they lived. It is a fact that all over the country where chalk pits were dug, labourers lived close by. Many a home still hails to the name of Chalk Pit Cottage.

Almost all early civilisations that had access to chalk made it, among other things, into lime for building. By heating the chalk (calcium carbonate), it drives out the carbon dioxide creating quicklime (calcium oxide). The quicklime would be ground and crushed into powder, packed into watertight barrels and stored in the lime sheds ready for local sale or shipment. Money was made from local Eastbourne folk who would come down to the hamlet to buy it. Lime is incredibly versatile with a thousand uses. Un-slaked or powdered lime could be sold for use in the pantry to preserve food and keep a work area dry. Lime wash was used to whitewash house walls and lime paste for softening leather. Caustic lime was used to cover corpses. In agriculture lime balanced acidic soil and improved newly broken land. In fact many tenant farmers were contractually obliged by the land owners to improve the soil that they worked. Spreading quicklime could be dangerous as it readily caught fire when exposed to water. More than one farmer's lime cart burnt to the ground when caught out in the rain. If you added water or sand to it, it became mortar or plaster for building. If the men added clay to the kiln, then raised the temperature of the lime mix, it became even more valuable cement.

Luckily, the rough weather that often stopped the fishing at Holywell also provided an essential ingredient in their lime making; wind. One of the by-products of lime burning is the deadly gas carbon monoxide, so lime production on windy shore-work days was ideal for the men. They built up layers of chalk and coal in the lime burning kilns, like a huge liquorice allsort. When the kiln was full it was lit and the fire slowly burned for about three days and nights. Eventually a magical transformation turned the chalk into the valuable resource of lime. To test the lime the workers would take out a lump and drop it into a barrel of water. If it fizzed, bubbled, and shattered it was ready.

It was essential when a young lad was taught the secrets of lime production that he was also taught about the dangers that invisibly surrounded it. Their very lives depended on what they were shown by their elders. For example, the lime powder would stick to the sweaty brows of the workers and react to the moisture, causing their skin to burn. There was also the deadlier carbon monoxide threat; although our ancestors never understood why some died after a night sleeping by the warmth of the kiln, they knew it happened. It was essential to scare the wits out of any young lad working the kilns. Stories of the devil coming to take the soul of any who fell asleep next to the lime kilns usually worked a treat, especially in winter, when the long cold nights would naturally draw the devil to the warmth.

The men of Holywell, living on their ancestral lands, were ideally situated to make the lime and transport it with their boats to the coastal towns, where it would be traded for goods, money and fuel for burning in their kilns and homes. The Holywell men regularly delivered lime to London by sea; a long and arduous journey, but well rewarded as the highest prices always came from the capital.

Later in the book I will tell you how it all came to an end. How the families that had lived, loved and worked on that land for generations, were forcibly moved because of progress, and the new boomtown that was growing on their doorstep.

Eastbourne Town Hall is undoubtedly one of the finest buildings in the town. The older illustration was made in the 1880's by S. Kirk. The building is immaculately maintained by our council, with the foundation stone being laid on 9 October 1884 by Lord Edward Cavendish. It was hoped that Queen Victoria would open the Town Hall in October of 1886 but she politely declined due to other pressing duties. The cost of building Eastbourne's premier property was £30,000 (can you imagine the costs today?) and there was a considerable outcry at the time about the Town Hall costing so much. However as the 130ft high clock tower was completed it became obvious that something very special was being created and the criticism died away. The clock by Gillet and Johnson was installed in 1892 and has been chiming ever since (only silenced during times of war). The renaissance style building was built by James Peerless builders from a design by Birmingham architect W. Tadman Foulkes.

CHAPTER 9

HOW IT ALL STARTED

The families that lived and worked on the chalk downland had little idea of how the hills were formed. It is a remarkable tale of evolution. When I look at our stunning South Downs it always amazes me that millions of years ago it was under the sea, and more than that, it was alive! Chalk is made up of countless aquatic creatures, plants and sealife in general; their bones, teeth, bodies and shells. As they perished they sank to the bottom of a great sea, slopping around in a huge primeval sludge. Think of a beach after a storm; washed up along the high tide line you'll see the remains of thousands of creatures, from weed and fish bones to sea shells. It is trillions of similar dead organisms that formed our chalk downlands.

But how did creatures from a mile deep become our soft green hills, known as the South Downs, hundreds of feet above sea level and run for almost 100 miles from Eastbourne westward? Let me explain; over unimaginable periods of time the lowest layer of decaying bodies on the seabed were compacted by pressure from the debris above, eventually becoming solid rock. Rock that we call chalk.

Something momentous then happened as our planet evolved.

Huge earth movements millions of years ago, formed the Alps as the shifting continental land masses of Europe, Asia and Africa collided in a slow moving traffic accident. As the land mass crashed together, some of it was forced upwards and the Alps were born. A by-product of these enormous land movements was a ripple effect that moved outward from the newly formed mountains. This ripple created valleys and hills as it went. Many miles to the north, the deep Sussex limestone seabed was heaved upwards into the elements. The sedimentary rock was then polished by time, the weather, sheep, and eventually man, into what is now our beautiful downland. The rest as they say, is history.

I love bringing our ancient past back to life and making sense of the world around us. Ninety million years of evolution boiled down into a few paragraphs!

Chapter 10
Town Building

Where once the whole of human life would have been set before your eyes at the Holywell Hamlet, now there are just the cold steel gates and a heavy silence. The last remains of that chalk quarry settlement has a sad tale to tell and it's all tied in with the building of Eastbourne.

There are still signs of the small community, like the few remaining apple and pear trees that dot the paths and the lumps of building material on the beach, but just about everything else, including the old families, has disappeared. Locals tell me that six good apple trees produce enough apples to make cider for a family for the year!

I have spoken to a distant relative from one of the families that were removed from the settlement. She had grown up with tales from that time. Like all the other families she was a commoner whose family had grown up on that special piece of land.

Was their eviction some sort of compulsory purchase? Were they little more than tenants? I shall tell you what I have dug up for it is a great piece of social history and part of how Eastbourne grew. But did she have the right tale? Legends and fables grow like mushrooms on a damp Autumn night. There is no doubt that her family home was destroyed along with all the others at Holywell, and the last ancient fishing village of early Eastbourne flattened, but why?

As we know, Eastbourne is relatively new, but the land on which the town now sits has been inhabited by humans for millennia. Quite often when 'new builds' take place they discover amazing finds. The biggest one locally was Shinewater, where they discovered a Bronze Age trading community. In 2017 archaeologists also carried out a dig on the old Parsons Field, next to Eastbourne Hospital (now Weavers Close), before commencing the new homes that are there now. In the field they found the remains of a Saxon community that had lived on the edge of what was once the sea, much like our hamlet at Holywell.

Victorian Eastbourne was originally conceived as a tourist town by the large and powerful landowning families of the area. The two most prominent ones were the large landowners, the Davies-Gilbert family, and William Cavendish, 2nd Earl of Burlington. There were others as well and many of our local streets are named after them; the Burtons, Gildredges, Selwyns and many more.

The Davies-Gilbert Family, who were instrumental in the birth of 'new' Eastbourne, owned a vast amount of land. They lived at Gildredge Manor in Gildredge Park. At one time the Grade II listed building was considered one of the finest Georgian buildings in the area. After Carew Davies-Gilbert died in 1913 the manor was sold to Eastbourne Council, which they used it to house an art gallery and museum dedicated to Alderman J C Towner (who had bequeathed enough money and art to get it started). The Towner Museum ran for over 80 years before being sold into private hands. After 2005 it was left vacant for several years and deteriorated badly, but luckily the current owners saved it and it is at present a sumptuous wedding venue.

The story of William Cavendish is straight out of a Jane Austen novel. In 1834, William, already fabulously wealthy, inherited even more land, estates and titles when his grandad, the 1st Earl of Burlington died. George Cavendish (The 1st Earl of Burlington) had married Lady Elizabeth Compton. Part of her estate was Compton Place in Eastbourne and the estates passed through the family line to the 6th Duke of Devonshire (known as the 'Bachelor Duke').

When the 6th Duke of Devonshire died in 1858, William Cavendish also inherited a dukedom. He now had the distinction of holding the highest aristocratic title in the land. William, (already the 2nd Earl of Burlington after his father had been killed in a carriage accident, missing the title because the 1st Earl was still living), was now also the 7th Duke of Devonshire. He became one of the wealthiest landowners in Britain, with estates stretching from Ireland to Scotland. Part of his estates now included Compton Place, which he made his seaside residence while in Eastbourne.

The tale of the 7th Duke is a fabulous one, full of drama and tragedy. He was an empire builder, everything from shipbuilding to railways, parks and baths. William Cavendish blazed a trail through 19th century Britain. He embraced the spirit of the age and brought work to countless numbers as he strove to build a better country. He outlived two of his sons (one being assassinated in Ireland) and most of his 11 siblings. He went on to see Britain become the largest empire the world had ever known.

Many years later, in the 1950's, after terrible losses in both World Wars, the Cavendish Family nearly lost everything with crippling death duties. Chatsworth, their family seat, remained empty for years, but through hard work, determination, and amazing leaps in land and property prices, they have since reclaimed their wealth.

Back in the 19th century, William Cavendish's dream to build a new town (that he had cherished since a child) was going to come true. The first and most important piece of civil engineering was to construct a sea wall to protect the new town.

James Berry proved to be the man who could not only design it, he could organize the massive movement of beach and chalk to achieve it. By 1847, utilising local labour (including the fishermen, who would later lose their homes due to the construction) James Berry produced a layered formation of stone, concrete and brick. Much of the foundation has survived to this day. It tamed Mother Nature and protected the flatlands and cornfields that would soon grow into a boomtown.

By 1858 William Cavendish, now not only an earl but the 7th Duke of Devonshire, attacked the idea of town building with vigour. This time he had the power and money to achieve his ambition. The Duke hired the best of the best, architects

Decimus Burton and Henry Currey (who was once Burton's pupil). Burton had already worked on Chatsworth and Kew Gardens and knew the Duke well.

The specialist town planners turned their eyes to the vast lands between the four main outlying boroughs of the area; East Bourne (now Old Town), South Bourne (the area around where the Town Hall now stands), the farms of Meads and the fishing hamlet at The Stade (which was down by the Sea Houses, not far from where the pier stands now). It would be mainly this area that would become the 'new' Eastbourne. Today East-bourne stretches all the way from Langney to Willingdon. Once these were very separate villages with most locals calling a visitor from one area to the other 'a foreigner'.

The Sea Houses and The Stade were the original attraction for early visitors to the area, being quoted as *unrivalled in point of delight and situation*. Interestingly in 1780, Prince Edward (Queen Victoria's father) had stayed in an old secluded windmill near the Sea Houses. It had been converted into a small guest house called the Round House. When the Round House was demolished in 1841, Roman mosaics were dis-covered under the foundations, probably from the ancient town of Anderida.

From the Sea Houses, coaches left daily for Brighton, Hastings and London, six days a week. The London coach left at 8am sharp. It was noted that with a stop for lunch and a good road, travellers could expect to arrive at the River Thames London Depot by 6pm, the very same day. However if the trip encountered difficulties (as they often did) occupants of the coach could expect an overnight delay. A two day trip to get to London was common!

I can imagine our 'new town builders' standing at some viewpoint on the Downs, staring down at the open spaces below them and talking about their ideas; how stunning hotels would stretch along the shoreline and how wide streets would join up the centre of their new town in a patchwork of elegance and Victorian style. Then superb schools, like Eastbourne College, would be built to attract a new generation of high-achieving classes.

Their plan was to take a space that held just a few thousand inhabitants, hardly changed for centuries, and build a boom-town. Little did they know (or could ever imagine) that the streets they made for horses, carts and carriages would one day find themselves packed with driverless carriages called motor cars. Or that coaches, with the capability to bring thousands from all over the country on summer breaks or 'tinsel & turkey' Christmas holidays, would need space to park.

However they were smart enough to know that for the town to prosper first they needed all the amenities. A public transport system was put in place. They secured rail, road and coach links, then they laid out a superb town, centering around wide boulevards and tree-lined streets, some of it based on Venetian and French designs.

Currey was a lover of Italian architecture, especially Venetian. Amongst the many buildings and structures that Currey designed was the stunning 150ft Winter Garden with a roller-skating rink inside. The Winter Garden was originally the entrance to Devonshire Park and looked suitably magnificent. The structure was mainly iron and glass. The stunning glass roof was later replaced with cheap zinc plated sheets and then Nuralite panels.

Currey based his superb design on Crystal Palace and several other major glass houses of the period, from Chatsworth to the Palm House at Kew Gardens, and even the Glass Pavilion in Buxton (one of the Duke's towns). The Winter Garden was completed in 1876 after Currey's original plan for housing was changed into a park by the Duke (when he realised that his visitors needed entertaining). The whole eleven and a half acres of Devonshire Park must have been a sight to behold. The entire area took several years to build and the park was eventually opened by the Duke on 1 July 1874. The indoor roller-skating rink in the Floral Hall was opened in 1875 with a demonstration by the inventor of the roller skate, J L Plimpton.

The Winter Garden and Devonshire Park have been the setting for many huge banquets, grand concerts, major tennis tournaments and much more. The Floral Hall even housed the Duke's permanent orchestra for a time. My personal favourite as a kid was the Saturday afternoon wrestling with visiting superstars like Giant Haystack and the 'sarf London tough guy' Mick McManus.

A huge reconstruction is currently underway of the whole park. The regeneration is the biggest in its 140 year history, costing over 54 million pounds. It will once again put Eastbourne at the forefront, not only for tourism but as a top cultural, sporting, conference and visitor destination. The grand opening is set for the summer of 2019, just as this book is going to press.

Currey's real masterpiece in my mind however, was the amazing reconstruction of the seafront. By cutting out the lower downland and moving unimaginable masses of chalk, he created a three-tiered promenade. Without modern machinery this was an audacious task, most of it undertaken with picks, shovels, barrows, brute force and gunpowder. However it would allow easy access from the sea all the way up to his new layout for Meads. Majestic hotels could then be built along the protected seashore, the first whopper being the Burlington Hotel along Grand Parade.

Interestingly Burlington was to be the name of the large new town before the Duke changed his mind and used the name of the old hamlet of Eastbourne (much of which we now refer to as Old Town).

This picture that I snapped in the summer of 2011 shows the appalling state that Gildredge Manor was allowed to fall into. Much of the lead from the roofs had been stolen, windows broken and boarded up. It would not have taken much more before it would have become a ruin, then like so many great properties, probably condemned and demolished.

In 2019, after a huge investment of time and money Gildredge Manor in Gildredge Park is once again standing alongside some of the finest Georgian properties in the county.

Devonshire Park built in 1874 was the pinnacle of the Duke's pleasure grounds. It showcased his dream of a vibrant tourist town, bustling with things to do and places to visit. The fabulous Winter Garden Floral Hall and Devonshire Park Theatre soon followed. In 1881 the South of England Grass Court Tennis Championships were first held in Devonshire Park.

'Among the many claims which Eastbourne puts forward for the favourable consideration of her visitors, none hold higher place than Devonshire Park. The Park epitomises the secluded atmosphere and select tone, which was the town's chief objective. Admission is sixpence, bath chairs are one shilling. Skating rinks are inside and out with a band in attendance,' (excerpt from a Daily Paper).

It is still possible to see Henry Currey's superb Winter Garden from the tennis courts behind the new Towner Gallery. Originally it was the entrance to Devonshire Park. It is well worth a visit as even now, lost amongst new developments, it stands out as an amazing piece of 19ᵗʰ Century architecture. Can you imagine what it must have looked like in its original coat of glass! The finest example I have seen of an original Winter Garden is in Glasgow. If ever you visit The People's Palace and Winter Garden at Glasgow Green you will see how fabulous they can look.

It is difficult to imagine today just how much the area around what we now call Eastbourne has changed, all in a relatively short time. At Shinewater you can still get a peek of the past and how this land looked to our ancestors for millennia. This reconstruction of an original Bronze Age dwelling (next to Sevenoaks Road) is stunning at sunset.

It is hard to believe but this is South Street circa 1870. A little different today!

Compton Place is one of the hidden gems of Eastbourne. It was originally an Elizabethan Jacobean mansion called Bourne Place, built by James Burton and remodelled centuries later by Colen Campbell (around 1726). Apparently, inside is an image or bust of him holding a compass and dividers. It has an amazing history entwined with dukes, lords and royalty. It was home to The Earl of Wilmington and the 5th Earl of Northampton until passing into the 7th Duke's estates. There has been a long list of distinguished visitors, from Capability Brown to King George VI. Along with the Davies-Gilbert family, the Duke of Devonshire used part of his lands to the south of Compton Place, to build his new town. John Davies-Gilbert and his son Carew Davies-Gilbert, had the same passions as the 7th Duke building a new town.

Compton Place was taken over in the 1950's by a London language centre. In 1954 they opened The Ladies Training College, 'finishing school for ladies'. Compton Place today, though still referred to as the LTC, is now a more traditional mixed language school called The Language Teaching Centre. Along with St Mary's Church in Old Town it is our only other Grade 1 listed building.

The Round House circa 1840 the year before it was demolished to make way for seafront improvements. George III's children had stayed on holiday there.

ABOVE: 1894. *The land had been cleared and the main promenades laid out as building work stretched up towards the Belgravia of Eastbourne, Meads. Looking east the promenade must have seemed more like a building site but looking west there was still plenty of clear land before All Saints Hospital.* BELOW: *Downs west.*

The Grade Two listed Burlington Hotel was the first premier residence for tourists, opening in 1851. Local historians say that Eastbourne was actually going to be named New Burlington before William Cavendish (the Earl of Burlington) realised he was going to inherit another amazing title and become the 7th Duke of Devonshire.

The seafront, running from the Burlington Hotel to the Queens Hotel, has changed little in the last 100 years. A visitor from 1912, as seen in this early Frith Collection picture, would recognise the hotels and Carpet Garden layout instantly today. The hotels are protected by strict building regulations and our local council which keeps an eye out for any unplanned alterations. When one of the hoteliers painted his lions gold he was immediately ordered to repaint them white or face the full wrath of the law. Hotel impresario Sheikh Abid Gulzar repainted all six of the lions outside his Albany Lions Hotel, leavings just the tips of their tails gold, in defiance.

The Sea Houses along Marine Parade are just a few of the buildings that stood before the main promenade of hotels were built. You can just see a glimpse of a few original features from the 1780's still there today, especially the sea flint on the rear of the buildings. Take a look at the cul-de-sac around the back and you will instantly step back into a Dickensian scene from long ago. Marine Parade formed part of what was known as The Stade, where the fishermen of Eastbourne lived and worked. It was the perfect attraction for visitors watching the local fishermen going about their daily duties. Looking at the architecture along Marine Parade you get a rare taste of 18th Century Eastbourne.

This is the original Stade before the artificial sea wall was built. Note the capstan in this image from 1850. These were used to haul in the larger trading vessels as well as the local fishing boats. Capstans were deadly and claimed several local fishermen's lives.

Grand Parade, circa 1909, showing the summer season in full bloom. The dream of the Duke would come true with countless visitors making the journey to his new town. Of course with the visitors came all the infrastructure that was needed to support them. Boomtown Eastbourne was still growing at a phenomenal rate.

Eastbourne seafront 1824

The Stade was the original fishing grounds and home of some of the early Eastbourne fishermen. It was one of the four first hamlets that were combined to make 'New Eastbourne'. As you can see the houses were almost on the seashore. The 'powers that be' needed to clear the area to continue with the sea wall that would protect the new hotels. This led to a bitter feud that had to be settled in court.

The Grand Hotel old and new with its 400 foot frontage. It is just one of the fabulous hotels lining Eastbourne's premier seafront. Local resident, William Earp, proposed the hotel at a cost of £50,000 in 1874. It was fully open by 1877 with over 200 rooms and only six lavatories! Chamber pots would be brought to you as requested by the hard working chambermaids, or the staff that the 'upper classes' brought with them. The hotel still dominates the seafront and has attracted visitors from Charlie Chaplin to Winston Churchill. The main 'grand entrance' by carriage was originally from the courtyard at the rear of the property.

CHAPTER 11

By the mid-Victorian era, trains, the marvel of the age were transforming travel and the country. Ease of travel made possible spending leisure time at destinations that were once out of reach. Where the trains stopped, hotels were needed.

On 14th May 1849, Eastbourne's first train arrived. The London, Brighton and South Coast Railway Companies train pulled in at midday and was heralded with much pomp and ceremony. It had chugged from Polegate into the new town of Eastbourne, stopping along Upperton Road. The train carried many important officials from the town and railway company. They say that the celebrations went on for over 18 hours. Most of the town turned out to see the new-fangled contraptions that ran on steel rails and could take you all the way to London in just a few hours.

The station was originally little more than a wooden shack. It was relocated in 1866 and again in 1872 (the same year as Eastbourne Pier was completed). It moved to its present location in 1886, probably because of Nicholas Whitley, who had drawn up extensive plans for the redevelopment of the Upperton area for the Gilbert Estates.

In 1851, huge gas storage facilities were brought in (where the noisy klaxon sounded twice a day at the end of the men's shifts). With gas came the wonder of street lighting to light the new boulevards. Lamplighters would light the streetlights each night and turn them out at dawn the following morning.

Bit by bit the ancient outlying boroughs from Langney to Willingdon were all connected by proper roads. The heart of the town would be centred on where the war memorial stands today, elegant rows of shops, restaurants, cafés and town houses all spreading out from its hub like a spider's web. The jewel in Eastbourne's crown would be a seafront to die for, bordered with parks, theatres and entertainment, from skating rinks to heated swimming pools.

A modern town, the height of sophistication, would be built to attract holiday makers, visitors, and new inhabitants. The Duke's 'pleasure grounds' would entertain visitors in the most lavish style. Eastbourne was about to hit the big time as the seaside holiday was born.

Visitors arrived, like the Swedish Nightingale, Jenny Lind (who Isaac Singer nearly named his first sewing machine after) and Alfred Lord Tennyson, who stayed at Sea Beach House (still a boarding house near Fusciardi's ice cream parlour at 39-40 Marine Parade). Eastbourne would go on attracting the rich and famous for the next 150 years.

The 1851 Eastbourne Census shows the population as 3,432 (with just 65 fishermen listed, though there were several more that were missed). In the next few years the town would grow beyond imagination. In 1861, a year after parliament required councils to provide clean water to residents, the population of the area had already doubled. By 1881 it was over 20,000 and by 1901 it had grown to over 40,000! Clean water had helped change the town.

Even the fishermen took advantage of this new opportunity, turning their trade into fishing and tourism, with boat trips around the new pier and lighthouse. Pleasure boating and bathing machines became their stable mates along with herring, mackerel, sprats, and cod.

Sea Beach House shown here was built in 1790. It was once 39 & 40 Marine Parade and used to look out straight onto the shingle beach then known as The Stade. No 39 Marine Parade (the part of Sea beach House with the name plaque on it) was once the home of Edward Allchorn and his family. It was Edward who first started and ran the Allchorn Pleasure Boats that plied their living along Eastbourne Promenade. William, his son took over after Edward's death in 1887.

The first railway station was little more than a wooden shack. When the station relocated the shack was moved to Wharf Road and became home to the station guard for several years. The second station was constantly improved to keep up with the massive expansion Eastbourne was undergoing. The superb Italianate yellow brick station that we see today was designed by F. D. Bannister and built in 1886. It has undergone steady improvements ever since.

This is Old Town in 1784, showing us one of the original hamlets all on its own. Old Town has some of the oldest properties in Sussex.

Old Town is where the River Bourne still bubbles to the surface at Motcombe Pond.

Old Town Post Office circa 1865 with St Mary's just visible behind.

94

CHAPTER 12

WATER, WATER EVERYWHERE
BUT NONE FIT TO DRINK!

The final resource that needed to be secured for the prosperity of the town, was the most precious one of all; water. Remember that's how we started our grand tale. Initially water came from supplies like the Bourne Stream in Old Town. The river, from which Eastbourne takes its name, bubbled to the surface at the Old Saxon settlement of Motcombe Pond. Bourne is Anglo Saxon for spring, river or stream. Countless places around our country, from Bournemouth to Ashbourne are all named after this invaluable commodity.

The Bourne was first mentioned in the Domesday Book (as Borne) and the stream still makes its way (mostly hidden now) from Old Town, through the Town Centre, all the way to the sea. It once came out in a large mouth on a shingle bank, I imagine much like the estuary of the Cuckmere today.

Motcombe Pond was made into a reservoir in 1844, but like the Hampden Park and later Bedfordwell waters, it proved problematic, erratic, and often distasteful. They suffered badly from dry spells and farm pollution from the surrounding fields and livestock. Remarkably when I was a kid in the 1960's, the

Star Brewery was still using the water from Motcombe for their great ale. I often took the risk of running through their yard on my way to Motcombe School each day. A kick up the backside was well worth the chance to stare into the open brewery doors and sniff their smelly potions.

Surprisingly, not everyone welcomed clean, safe water. Breweries were doing a roaring trade, selling weak beer, after Parliament had imposed the Gin Act Tax of 1736. This tax stopped gin and other spirits from being the main drink of the working classes. It sounds impossible today but a good proportion of the British workforce were turning up for work under the crippling influence of alcohol. Weak beer was a far safer and more productive alternative!

The eventual arrival of clean water spelt the end of the domination of the breweries that had been steadily expanding since the arrival of hops to Winchelsea in the 12th Century. In London alone (where the first public drinking fountain opened in 1859) over 12,000 small breweries closed as a result of clean water becoming available! Even the Tower of London had an astounding 21 pubs! And we thought micro-breweries were a new fad! From 1801 to 1851 the population of London exploded with over a million extra inhabitants. In 1858 the Capital's pollution was so bad due to the mass of raw sewage flowing down the River Thames, that it became known as 'the year of the Great Stink'. It was partly due to the 'Great Stink' that the sewage system (still in use today) was constructed.

Even tea, traditionally an afternoon beverage that was safe as it used boiled water, saw a sharp decline (until decades later it became the nation's favourite breakfast pick-me-up). Tea sales had initially soared after the British transported tea from China to India and planted countless thousands of acres of Camellia bushes across the landscape. This had dropped the price within range of the masses, making it our most popular drink since the Victorian times.

In 1859, by Act of Parliament, the Eastbourne Waterworks Company (founded and controlled by the 7th Duke of Devonshire) was formed to deal with the growing problem of water supply and demand in the new town.

George A. Wallis, a young man with a huge talent was hired by the company. George was only 20 at the time and took charge of the water, drainage and sewerage for the town. Wallis also designed the superb twisting road to Beachy Head that we now call Upper Duke's Drive. The winding ascent was so smooth that travelling the 476 feet up to top of the hills seemed almost effortless. He excelled at his job and his tireless efforts ensured that one of the main problems of a growing town would be overcome. Wallis went on to run the Duke's building estates in Eastbourne and in 1864 he was appointed the Duke of Devonshire's main land agent. In 1867 he oversaw the opening of Eastbourne sewer.

Wallis eventually became the first Mayor of Eastbourne in 1883, after the parish had become a town. Intense lobbying by the parish, and all the major parties concerned, had successfully obtained the grant of a royal charter. Here we finally see the birth of modern Eastbourne.

Let's step back a little and see how the United Kingdom dealt with the problem of safe drinking water. Science in 19th century Britain was discovering just how many lethal pollutants were carried in water. Typhoid and cholera had been sweeping across the country, leaving a path of death and destruction in their wake. At first it was not clear that it was spread by humans in waste water. For centuries the belief was that killers, like typhoid, cholera, plague, and even malaria, travelled in the ether on vapours called miasmas. However, authorities were noticing that communities drinking from unpolluted deep water wells, survived relatively untouched.

Business moguls like Sir Titus Salts, could see the financial gain in keeping his workers healthy. In an extraordinary action he moved his entire workforce out of Bradford, building a new village next to his huge textile mill, Salt's Mill. His workers had clean water and a longer life. Astonishingly, before the Factories Act of 1833, which forced bosses to limit children aged 9 to 13 to work no more than 54 hours a week, the average life expectancy in Bradford at the time was under 20! Now if you wanted a longer life the place to head for was Salford, hardly a mile from the centre of Manchester. There the average life expectancy was a whopping 37! The great news was that at Salt's new village of Saltaire the life expectancy tripled.

Previously, as we mentioned, weak beer had been drunk as a safer alternative to dirty water, but in a modernising, industrial world, that was no longer an option. In Ireland, in the 1840's, already suffering greatly from poor harvests and famine, cholera killed over 50,000 people. Scotland had the brilliant solution of pumping water into the growing cities from their abundant lochs. For example, 3,000 workmen built the necessary tunnels, viaducts and aqueducts to supply 90 million gallons of crystal clear water each day to Glasgow alone.

In 1848 The Public Health Act was brought in to try and stop the cholera epidemic killing thousands more as it swept across Britain. The act aimed to improve the sanitary conditions of the booming towns, where the epidemics were rife. By 1850 John Snow in London had proved beyond all doubt that it was contaminated water that spread cholera. Simply by improving the water supply and drainage, lives could be saved.

Combining water, sewerage, paving, drainage and environmental health, all under one local board of health, the Government could control the developments of towns in a far more organised and healthier way.

Those that could afford it bought new-fangled water filters. One of the large companies at the time was situated in The Strand in London, The London & General Water Purifying Company. They used 'animal charcoal' filters to successfully remove pollutants and germs from the water; even Queen Victoria used them at Osborne House, as did the Prince of Wales at Sandringham. Another popular make (if you had the money) was the Saludor Water Purifier made by Cheavin's. They used a combination of charcoal, ceramics, fine meshes and silver to filter the water. Unfortunately if you did not keep up the regular maintenance on them, they could become just as dangerous as the local river outside!

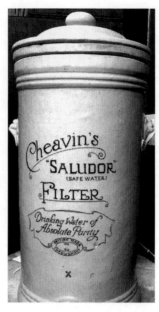

Some of the grand hotels in London like The Savoy sunk their own artesian wells deep into the ground. These free flowing bore holes produced fresh clean water for their customers.

Back in Eastbourne local laundries were booming, cleaning the linen from the growing number of hotels, as well as many of the well-off houses and countless private schools that were being built. Seven days a week, horse and carts collected laundry from all over our town. The laundries had a constant problem obtaining clean water. Some, like Beach Laundry, experimented with flat roofs to trap rainwater, which they stored in huge underground vaults (that apparently still exist near Eshton Road under the nursing home).

With all this impressive town planning, by 1874, the Duke was winning the race for wealthy tourists against his main competitors along the south coast (which were Hastings, and the Prince Regent's favourite bolt hole, Brighton). Experts had started to identify sources of clean water, and plans were well underway to exploit Eastbourne's natural resources.

By 1881, Eastbourne Waterworks Company started sinking wells and building a superb state-of-the-art pumping station at Bedford Wells, along the back of what is now Bedfordwell Road. It is near Whitley Bridge, named after the Cornish engineer Nicholas Whitley, who had developed Seaside and the Upperton areas for the Gilbert Estates.

Bedfordwell was an ancient water source that had been used for millennia and certainly documented from the 14th Century. Besides Motcombe and Holywell it was one of the main water supplies for the early inhabitants of the area. It was hoped that massive investment in the latest technology would allow more water to be pumped for the booming town.

The stunning pumping station was designed by Henry Currey with the engineering overseen by the future mayor, George A. Wallis, all under the keen eye of the Duke. Henry's daughter, Ada, laid the foundation stone in 1881 that can still be seen on the south side of the property. The building was finished two years later in 1883, the same year Wallis became Mayor of Eastbourne. The pumps went on line with a grand opening by the future king and his wife, the Prince of Wales and Princess Alexandra. The two huge rotary-pump beam engines were named in their honour as Prince and Princess. When the Cornish type boilers (behind the pump rooms) were at full pressure, the 150ft high chimney stack would belch out black smoke and the pumps pushed out an amazing five million gallons of water a day. A siding from the main railway was put in for special trains to deliver coal straight to the boiler room.

However, once again the water proved problematic. The lowlands were rich in grazing and in certain climatic events the 'taste' filtered through to the wells. We all know what it is like when we drink something awful, don't we! Reliable sources of water needed to be found so that the new town could maintain its hard earned reputation for excellence. After all, Eastbourne's standing as 'The Empress of Watering Places' was at stake.

'No watering place on the southern coast is fairer than Eastbourne; none is so elegant in the dispositions of its attractions. Eastbourne is indeed in all her attributes, a graceful dame, whose beauty is enhanced by every kind of becoming ornament.'

The Daily Telegraph, December 1893

The problem was that the oval wells at Bedfordwell were only about 43 feet deep and could become easily contaminated. By 1895, after countless attempts to solve the problems at Bedfordwell, the pumps were deemed useless. Even after unimaginable expense, the beam engines ground to a halt. They were apparently dismantled and taken to Friston Pumping Station.

The building was used for a few years by Eastbourne Council before falling into disrepair, but the brilliant quality of the Victorian workmanship ensured that the pump house survived as a disused monument. The listed Bedfordwell Pumping

Station and the surrounding area is currently under a massive redevelopment. The old pump house is being restored and changed into some form of residence. I can't wait to see inside. Ever the nosey dog, I once crept in, only to find an empty cavernous hole; the outer walls were held together with enormous steel girders. After the pumping station was closed, and the great pumps dismantled, all that was left was an empty home for rats, cats and pigeons.

With the closure of Bedfordwell, the small fishing hamlet of Holywell needed to be secured so that the town could use all of the ancient, deep chalk wells. The water, naturally filtered by the chalk downland, was clean and crisp. No better drinking water could possibly be found.

In 1896, plans to obtain complete control over the prized fresh water at Holywell (that William Cavendish had started 60 years earlier) were proceeding nicely. This time there would be no chance of contamination. The 8th Duke had begun by purchasing some of the land from the fishermen who were willing to sell, but the rest of the fishermen were not so lucky. Those that refused to leave Holywell would have to be forced.

On 17th November 1896, Eastbourne Waterworks Company put forward further proposals for Acts of Parliament. In several bills they put forward all the necessary paperwork to secure water from Jevington and Folkington, Willingdon, Friston, Paradise Woods (above The Royal Golf Course), and finally the jewel in the crown, Holywell. They needed Parliament to sanction and confirm the 'purchase by compulsion' of houses, land, water, property, rights and privileges; everything that was needed for Eastbourne's future water supply. This would allow local laws to be overridden. Amazingly it can still be applied for today.

The water company was soon armed with all the power it needed to remove, by force if required, anyone or anything in their way. Eastbourne's need for water outweighed any obstruction. I can find no mention of what compensation was to be paid to the casualties. It was probably worked out individually for each purchase with the authority to compulsory purchase land, needed to secure a permanent and reliable supply of water for the town, the new Duke moved fast. So successful were these plans for a water supply that it was not until the 1970's that another reservoir (Arlington) was needed.

In 1897, six years after the 7th Duke of Devonshire had died and the same year that his last remaining son (the 8th Duke) became Mayor of Eastbourne, the Friston Waterworks came on line. The water was pumped via a trunk-main (buried twenty feet down), all the way to Beachy Head, then down to the town. Supplies were better, but the town was growing faster and faster, its population exploding as the dreams of William Cavendish and the Davies-Gilbert family came true.

By 1948 the daily water needs of Eastbourne was over 1·75 million gallons a day, supplied mainly by Friston (it had a 1·5 million gallon capacity), St Annes Road Reservoir (3·5 million gallon capacity) plus the Paradise, Holywell and Beachy Head Reservoirs (with over 7 million gallons capacity).

At last the water supply for Eastbourne was done and dusted, and the town building could continue. We are now going to look at the families who lived at Holywell and what happened to them.

Mote Combe or Motcombe pond, where the original Bourne Stream springs to life. It was converted into a basic reservoir in 1844 but failed to supply clean water.

Communal pumps and fountains were one of the only ways to obtain water. Many a town grew around the pump which became more and more ornate. Interestingly, even as late as 1880 water in Eastbourne was supplied by water carriers (mainly children) and pumped up to standpipes and drinking fountains in public places. One example of a 19th Century public drinking fountain still exists. It was found in a basement and renovated before being placed not far from Eastbourne Pier, outside Fusciardi's Café along the promenade.

The drinking fountain outside Fusciardi's Café was donated to Eastbourne in 1865 by Elizabeth Curling for public use. When I was a kid it was located on the corner of Seaside and Pevensey Roads (opposite the Leaf Hall, built as a workmen's club by William Leaf). Thousands came out to see its official opening.

Devonshire Park & Baths Company Ltd. The Devonshire Baths were designed by G. A. Wallis, the first mayor of Eastbourne and the Duke of Devonshire's agent. They opened to an expectant public on 1st April 1874. The structure is none too impressive because most of the amazing work was below ground. The two main pools were separated, the larger being for men only and the smaller for the women. Family bathing was allowed three times a week. Devonshire Mansions now sits where the baths were.

With a massive building programme underway, each time the Duke visited he would have been taken on the 'tour' to see all the new buildings.

Here is the same view just a few years later with the new hotels all lining the promenade. The Duke specifically put in place orders and restrictions prohibiting shops and the sales of goods along the seafront. They are still in place today. Presently only the Lifeboat Museum on the seafront has been allowed to use its premises as a shop.

The Italianate Grade II listed Devonshire Park Theatre was designed by Henry Currey and completed in 1884. Some say it is the finest small 19th Century theatre in England. It was one of the final pieces in the Duke's Pleasure Grounds to entertain visitors. The theatre designer Frank Matcham made vast improvements to the theatre in 1903 and it has hardly changed since. The stairways were fireproofed and the towers housed huge water tanks in case of emergencies. Amazingly the small theatre can easily hold a thousand people with seating for 936.

Bedfordwell Pumping Station has been derelict for many years. After countless delays work started in late 2018 for the impressive monument to be converted into dwellings.

The 7th Duke
as an old man

William Cavendish
was an astonishing
character full of
determination, vision,
will-power and drive.
His foresight took an
old valley full of farms,
outlying villages, and
small parishes and
created a town fit for
royalty.
Would it be possible
today?

The Honourable Spencer
Compton Cavendish,
8th Duke of Devonshire
(1833-1908) spent
most of his life in politics,
taking over, in 1875,
as leader of the Liberal Party
from William Gladstone.
Spencer, as the eldest son,
watched over his father's
dreams and completed
much of his work.
This portrait by
Alexander Bassano
hangs in the
National Portrait Gallery.

CHAPTER 13

THE END OF HOLYWELL HAMLET

Once again we are back to Holywell, that insignificant area on the edge of Eastbourne that few tourists visit. Yet it is a definitive point in our story of town building.

Many fisher folk, like the Boniface and Prodger families, had lived in the Fisherman's Cottages at Holywell for generations, naturally claiming ancestral rights to the land. A few more sturdy fishermen actually lived in Meads and made the daily walk down to the sea. They had all made their living from the chalk pits, farmland and sea that surrounded them. Rumours say that even a little smuggling went on when times were hard (this supposedly kept the customs men busy).

With the currents around our coastline being some of the most dangerous in the country, fishermen would still risk their lives for little reward. They were the perfect smugglers, even with excise officers ready to pounce, they knew every tide, every shallow beach and back path. Fishermen went to amazing lengths to hide their 'special' goods: barrels of fish often hid skeins of silk, ankers (small casks of booze) or bottles of brandy. Rolled up nets could hide a bounty of baccy and port inside, and tea would be stored in plain sight under heaps of coal or layers of sailcloth.

Of course the local pub was the first retail outlet and the biggest customer for the smugglers. A fit young fisherman could strap two ten gallon barrels of brandy or 'tubs' to him and walk silently through the night to the back of the inn door. The cost to the fishermen was high as maritime records show that our coasts are littered with the wrecks of sunken ships.

There is one tale that the Holywell Fishermen were always repairing one of their boats over some old planks behind one of the cottages. It all looked innocent enough but underneath was a huge hole where they placed all their smuggled goodies. Funnily, it is also said that the coastguards had known all about it!

The families that lived by their seaside home must have been much like the Celts who inhabited the same area around 500BC; their life, work, sleep and play, all unfolding between the curving moon and endless tides.

Eastbourne had been desperate for clean drinking water and after the failure of the Bedfordwell Pumps the decision was taken to move in on Holywell. In 1896, using the excuse of 'in the interests of public health', the local authorities acted to secure the water catchment area.

The tale goes (and it may just be an old fisherman's yarn) that one perfectly timed day, when just the women of the cottages were home, bailiffs arrived with papers. They went into each cottage reading out the documents to the homeowner.

I have been told that because of poor schooling most of the women could neither read nor write. They had to take the bailiffs at their word. Allegedly, they were told that if they did not make their mark on the paperwork, they and their families could be evicted on the spot, by whatever force needed. However, if they signed they could have a period of grace. As most of the men were away, fishing or ferrying lime to London along the coast, the women had to make a decision. Reluctantly, each made their mark on the paperwork for their cottage and piece of land. Once finished, the bailiffs left and the bewildered women hoped that was the end of it. But it was just the beginning of a carefully orchestrated plan.

What the women may not have fully understood was that they were signing away the rights to their land and property forever, land that their families had inhabited for centuries.

The Holywell story really falls into three parts or phases, as the fishermen from Holywell did not all move in one go. They moved in three distinct periods. The final one was in 1896 but the first move was nearly seventy years earlier.

A parcel of land at the hamlet had already passed to the Cavendish family as early as 1827, when the Cavendish Estate bought a plot from Jacob Wood. I believe a small (but essential for legal purposes) peppercorn rent of one shilling may have been charged for the use of the land. From that time on, some of the families may have been little more than crofters, working the land but not owning it.

I talked to Bob Wood. He still lives locally and he remembers well how his dad could sniff out trouble at sea. More than once he would make the fishermen pack up and head for home in calm waters, only for them to find that by the time they reached shore a nasty wind and wave had picked up. "We would all be complaining that we had to stop fishing, but by the time we were nearly home we were as grateful as could be. I never did know how he could tell and never asked. He just seemed to know."

The land purchased by the Cavendish Estate shows an interesting fact. As a youngster, William Cavendish had stayed with his grandparents at Compton Place. It must have been obvious to him even then, that water was the first essential ingredient for a town, and that the cleanest water was at Holywell. As a teenager his grandparents may have even talked of a new town. It is possible that they had prepared the way for that dream with that first purchase of land at Holywell in 1827. So Jacob Wood, and maybe others, had moved first in that year.

Phase two. More families moved in 1840 when the first pumping station was built at Holywell. The latest Cornish style pumps, developed for the West Country tin mines were brought in and placed over the wells at Holywell. With room so tight on the small plateau of land at Holywell, the fishermen that made way for the building of the pumping station had to move. They moved to the Marine Parade area of town, then known as Reed's Cottages and Hurst's Cottages, near Burfield Road and The Leaf Hall today.

In reality the entire settlement had been constantly crumbling away, as the sea nibbled at its edges. As the fishermen's land fell into the water, the boats were harder to reach, the nets and fish heavier to cart up the steep slopes, and the chalk and lime tougher to transport. The precious wells had to be protected at all costs.

Extensive defences all proved useless against the raging sea and never-ending drag of the tides. The defences also took a huge amount of time and effort for the fishermen to maintain. The fishermen were always fighting a losing battle against what we now call Long Shore Drift, where beach and shingle is clawed away and deposited further along the coast. If you search the beach at Holywell you can still see the remains of their efforts to protect their homes.

The third and final phase was in 1896, when it was decided that because of the failure of the Bedfordwell pumps, (caused by the surrounding pollution seeping into the water) that no risks of pollution would be taken with Holywell. The families, and the possible pollution they could pose living above the clean water, had to go!

However, the people of the small fishing community were not leaving their ancient homes before sorting out their future. Now, those fish wives at Holywell may not have had a great schooling, but they were as sharp as their filleting knives. They knew that there were rows of superb terraced houses being built to the east of town, complete with crazy luxuries. As hard as it was to believe all the new houses had a tap in the back yard, next to the loo, that produced clean water anytime they needed. More amazing still, some had 'the miracle of the age,' instant gas lighting. No more smelly oil lamps propped up on shelves in draughty wooden cottages. No more trips to the well for water. No more hard slogs up and down the hills to get to market or into town to sell their fish.

The new part of town along Seaside (that became known by some as the East End) was growing fast and there were already many fishing families down that side of town. It was there that the last fishing families of Holywell had set their sights on. The new homes that had been built were to house the influx of working families needed to support the businesses and hotels of our new boomtown.

If the Holywell families played their cards right they would have their pick of the houses, and permission granted for their fishing boats on the beach, including all the paraphernalia that went with them, from lobster pots to net sheds. It was well known that the 'new' Duke could be a good friend to the fishing families if they were cooperative. William Cavendish had often played with the fishermen's children on his visits to Eastbourne as a child, when he would stay with his grandparents at Compton Place. He knew many of the men by their nicknames meant to confuse the authorities when smuggling.

Don't forget, Eastbourne was being built mainly as a tourist town. The homes and hotels needed the fishermen and their daily fish. What they did not need was more scandal, bad press, and court cases.

The Holywell families would also have been well aware of what had happened to their friends and relatives down on the shingle beach at The Stade a few years earlier. We shall be discussing that in more depth shortly. The fishermen were all shoved off their land after a huge legal struggle that failed. Remember the golden rule! The one with the gold makes the rule.

The families also knew that the new town of Eastbourne was growing at an incredible rate and there would be no stopping progress, nor the compulsory purchase upon them. All that they could do was to hold out for the best deal. The powerful land owners and ruling families, from Dukes to Lords, were unstoppable. They had united to build a town fit for royalty from which they could all profit.

Shortly after the visit by the authorities at Holywell, all the inhabitants were moved off the land. Huge steel gates were then erected along the old Holywell road. The area was locked away from public access and spiked railings were installed along the top path from Whitbread Hollow to block any way back to the properties.

Workmen then moved in. They demolished all the little white cottages. They destroyed the picket fences, vegetable gardens and the net drying sheds. They pulled down the smoking sheds where mackerel, herring and cod had been salted and hooked up for generations. They levelled the lime bunkers, leaving nothing but rubble and their original pumping station sheds.

Later they installed more pumps and machinery on the land (directly above the ancient water hidden in the chalk). And so Holywell Pumping Station was born with a legend tagged to its tail.

We will probably never know what actually happened, unless some old fisherman's diary turns up. But before you stand up and shout for justice, there is another version of the events.

The facts that we do know are that officials did turn up at the hamlet, and we know that the fishermen and their families left shortly after. This version goes that when all was agreed at Holywell a deal was struck. The families signed over their homes and rights before moving to the new homes provided for them at Fisherman's Green, all without too much aggravation. Still, it must have been a sad day as the last cart rolled up the chalk path and the last boat pulled away from the beach at Holywell.

This more peaceful version of events of the move might not be such a dramatic story, but far more practical and amicable to all parties.

I remember old man Boniface, who had retired after a life at sea. His family was one of the Holywell families that had moved. He would spend his sunny days selling his paintings along the seafront. Usually dressed in a straw boater and smart but worn waistcoat, he would sit and paint seaside scenes of Eastbourne Pier or the coast running towards Holywell. Then he would sell them to the tourists for a small fee. If you had the time he would tell you stories of how the beach was mined and wired up during the war and the pier cut in half before being strung with bombs, so that it could be blown up in the event of a landing attempt.

Mother Nature was the only real winner at Holywell, as the sea has since reclaimed much of the land where the original fishing families had lived. Whatever the truth, by 1900 the Holywell Families were in their new homes down the coast, water was secured, and peace came to Eastbourne.

Coastal erosion has taken its toll and today little is left of the large plateau that the Holywell Families once lived on.

Circa 1885, these are some of the last images taken before families like the Boniface's moved down into the town. It shows the complete hamlet was far larger than people imagined. Also notice the large square building in the foreground in one image. That was the new pumping station with steam pumps and the coal sheds behind. You will also see from the two images that some of the cottages have already gone, showing that a few families must have moved before the final closure. Also notice the erosion of the foreshore once the fishermen no longer bothered to protect it.

Today there is hardly a trace left of the once bustling hamlet. Without the fishermen's effort much of the ground has eroded back towards the cliff face. The rest has simply overgrown. You can see that the hamlet just before its closure was far larger than the painting that Amos had painted earlier (which was looking west). This shows a large community with all that was needed to survive. This is one of the only images that I have come across to show most of the Holywell Hamlet.

CHAPTER 14
THE STADE

In the last chapter I mentioned The Stade. Luckily we have a lot more information about the original fishing families that lived there, and how they were moved out of the way for the Duke's new town. They were not living over valuable water but they were right in the middle of the Duke's plan for a seaside town

A few years before the evictions at Holywell, as the Promenade had expanded eastward, the authorities needed to shovel the last resisting fishermen off the land that they had used for centuries. This land, just east of the pier, was known as The Stade. It was one of the original hamlets of the area.

Eastward from the pier and the Queens Hotel, our town changes from grand Victorian hotels to smaller boarding houses, guest houses, and sea houses. Henry Currey and the Duke had the idea to split Eastbourne into sections, with the workers or 'service staff' living east of the main town, in long terraced rows of purpose-built houses. Henry Currey had designed the impressive hotel as a natural barrier to divide the classes.

It was opposite the imposing Albion Hotel along Marine Parade where the majority of the fishing families still worked. The amazingly beautiful Albion (currently The Shore View Hotel) was the home of Lord Ashburnham when in town. When it became a hotel, it was the first hotel in Eastbourne to have electricity. It has gone through many periods of poor maintenance and closures, but with a massive renovation project in 2014 it has survived. I remember well the council forcing one owner to paint the dilapidated building that dates from the 1820's. I was also told that it was the very first hotel to have a telephone. It had the number Eastbourne One. The beaches opposite the hotel were strewn with fishing paraphernalia, pots and ropes, nets and boats. It was a working beach with tar greased rollers running down to the shore for the boats to be hauled up and down on. It was mucky, smelly, and not what the Duke wanted his visitors to be confronted with.

Land had been prepared for the fishing families further down the coast, on the other side of the Redoubt Fortress. Their mess and smell would be well away from the prim and proper visitors. There would be no drunken sea shanties sung on the Duke's new promenade if he could help it!

The Davies-Gilbert Estates, and the Duke of Devonshire, had enticingly supplied free land for the fishermen to move to. The fishermen were wary of leaving their ancestral property, even though it was only a few hundred yards down the coast, and they dug their heels in, refusing to budge.

Initially the authorities pulled funding from the maintenance of the fishermen's beaches to encourage the move. The Stade was allowed to fall into disrepair, the groynes were left to rot, the shingle beach 'sea wall' was not reinforced and the capstans not maintained. The capstans were the huge pulley mechanisms that helped to haul the vessels out of the water. Capstans were lethal and have claimed the lives of several Eastbourne fishermen. In 1917 William Langley was killed by one when a spoke cracked him around the head. Leonard Hide also went the same way in 1921, dying instantly.

Back at The Stade the lack of maintenance led to the fishermen's beach being open to the elements and dangerous to work. However, the stubborn fishermen, reluctant to lose their ancient rights, still refused to move.

On 17 June 1879 the Eastbourne Improvement Bill came before The House of Lords. Arguments were heard on both sides but there was no way the fishermen were ever going to win. The new area had been prepared for the fishermen and, as much as they squirmed, shouted, and wriggled, the course of Eastbourne history was set. All the fishermen's arguments were pulled apart and the bill flew through the Select Committee. The daily papers murmured that the House of Lords was backing one of their own. In reality it did not matter. Once the law was against the fishermen, they were fighting a losing battle.

Back home on The Stade, the fishermen stuck to their gunnels, but as we have seen all around the world, 'progress' was not going to be stopped by a few stubborn men protecting their ancient lands. By June of 1880 things came to a head. The Eastbourne Local Board declared, "Any boats, tackle or equipment still on the area once known as The Stade, after 8 June 1880 would be removed by force. Any damage occurring would not be reinstated!"

Reluctantly, and rather noisily, the fishermen moved the short distance to the other side of The Redoubt Fortress. The sea defences, promenade and sea wall progressed eastward, culminating at what became known as Splash Point at the Redoubt Fortress (due to the huge waves that crashed onto the sea wall before the new shingle beach was built up late in the 20th Century).

It wasn't all bad news. The fishermen had put up such a great fight that the land they had secured further down was theirs forever. No sea wall would be erected as long as fishing boats and huts remained on the beach. They would be able to ply their trade unhindered by the authorities. I've been told that there was another little clause added in the fine print which stated something like, if ever fishing stopped along the 'new' fishing zone, the land and its rights would revert back to the Gilbert and Devonshire estates. In fact I have since been told that most of the original fishing families have let go of their rights, with possibly only two families still holding on to that charter. Watch out boys, that is prime development land worth its pebbles in gold!

The roads off Seaside still reflect the old trades: Fisherman's Square, Fisherman's Green, Tideswell Road, Marine Road, Coastguard Square, Beach Road, Channel View Road and so on. Just off Latimer Road, at 10 Eshton Road, was where some of my wife's family, the Reeds lived (opposite the Allchorns). If you look at where Treasure Island is today, with the car parks and tennis courts (Penhale Road area), that is where the nets were repaired after being boiled in a solution of tree bark (which preserved them). Then they were hung out between dozens of strong poles to dry. By 1923, some of the unprotected area of Fisherman's Green was suffering from the town's expansion and grabbed back by the Council to be made into the tennis courts that we see today.

I mentioned right back at the beginning of this tale a few of the original families of the area. However, we must not forget the names of the fishermen who made up one of the most important parts of the old area sucked up into our 'new' town. There were around 30 main fishing families in the old area. The Allchorns, Bonifaces, Bucklands, Coles, Erridges, Hides, Huggetts, Pococks, Prodgers, Woods, Reeds, Chesters, Hardys, Becketts, Pages, Vines, Tutts, Sayers, Swains, Sewells, Clarks, Simpsons, Harts, Mocketts, Bates, Youngs, Colsticks, Jacksons, Stanbridges, and more.

Most of the fishermen had nicknames like Charles 'Bones' Hide or 'Pincher' Hide, (which were originally used to confuse the excise men). The tradition carries on to the present day entwined seamlessly in with the lifeboats. 'Tinker' Novis, a builder by day, would run to the sound of the explosions that called the lifeboatmen to an emergency (before mobile phones). He was the 'bowman', responsible for standing on the bow of the lifeboat and shooting the ropes over to the boat in distress. In the summer, if building work was slow and the weather right, he hired a few small boats along the front out to holidaymakers. His family still live a stones throw from the sea today. Several families still plough their watery trade on the high seas. Bob Page's old fish shop, currently the Southern Head Fishing Co, by the Lifeboat Station, still sells wonderful 'sea produce', pulled fresh from the waves each day.

When the rockets went up to summon the men to 'man the lifeboat' it wasn't just the men who ran to the lifeboat. Marlene Parkes (née Reed) remembers clearly that many children would run with the men, dashing down to Fisherman's Green and the lifeboat station. It was always first come first served with the lifeboat. Once they had enough crew they were off. Every second waiting could cost lives. Those still running for the boat from further afield would miss it. The kids would watch with tremendous excitement as the men jumped aboard and the lifeboat was launched down to the water with an explosion of sea and surf. Brilliantly heroic stuff that still goes on today, saving lives upon the sea.

A seaman's mission (called The Bethel) was also built off Royal Parade. The small wooden building, near the fish market was open most of the time to allow men coming in from the boats at night to get a good meal and hot drink. The two room building was used partly as a mission, and partly as a social club, where fishermen met when stormy weather stopped the boats putting out to sea. Eventually it was replaced with the Fisherman's Club that stands there today.

The Albion Hotel, along Marine Parade, is currently called the Shore View Hotel. It is where the majority of the fishing families once worked the beach. The amazingly beautiful Albion was initially the summer residence of Lord Ashburnham. When it became a hotel it was one of the first to have electricity and I've been told the first to have a phone, with the brilliant number, Eastbourne 1.

Here I am with the wonderful Betty Langley (now 91). Betty once lived in Tideswell Road and still lives in Eastbourne. You can see I haven't quite mastered the 'selfie'.

'Earlydoors', Harry Allchorn in September 1942 holding Annette Reed & Marlene Cottington outside 8 & 10 Eshton road. Harry was exempt from war duties due to being a fisherman, although later they became more involved in the tourist industry with holiday day trips round the lighthouse. Harry's nickname was from working on the door at the Hippodrome Theatre for the afternoon matinee. The Allchorn family have long been associated with the old fishing families of Eastbourne.

Charlie 'Bones' Hide in 1884 wearing his bravery medals for his major part in rescuing the crew of the New Brunswick in 1883. The New Brunswick had been wrecked in a sudden squall after dark on Sunday 25 November. An epic struggle was undertaken to drag the Eastbourne Lifeboat, the William and Mary, over the South Downs and launch it by Birling Gap, in time to rescue the crew. 'Bones' was one of the great characters from the old Hide fishing family. He seemed to be in trouble with the law and a local hero all at the same time. Fearless and brave, quick to anger and quick to forgive, 'Bones' seemed to encompass all the qualities of the tough Eastbourne seamen.

Jesse Huggett 1849-1900. Jesse took over as coxswain of the Eastbourne Lifeboat, the William & Mary, from Charlie 'Bones' Hide (until his untimely death in 1900). Each Christmas Jesse would collect gifts from the townspeople and take them out to the crew of the Royal Sovereign Lightship. Notice the incredibly basic cork life jacket that Jesse is wearing.

25th Nov 1883

This image of the lifeboat crew in 1883 is one of the most famous ones. They were the crew that carried out the herculean task of dragging and carrying their lifeboat, the William and Mary, over the South Downs before launching it at Birling Gap, to rescue the crew from the Norwegian barque the New Brunswick. The first Mayor of Eastbourne, G.A.Wallis, presented the men with medals and a gift of £4 each man. A considerable sum in 1883.

This is a photo of our current lifeboat crew taken in 2019. They have that unique and heroic quality needed to rush into danger, to put their own lives at risk to save others. Image courtesy of Carl Pocock, Lifeboat Operations Manager.

Here I am with my old friend Carl Pocock, Lifeboat Operations Manager (LOM). Carl has the huge responsibility of managing the operational activities at the lifeboat station. He authorises the launch of the lifeboat and day-to-day management of the station. He may get buzzed at three in the morning and have to make life changing decisions. We are standing on the current lifeboat, the £2.7m RNLB Diamond Jubilee, a Taymar-class all-weather lifeboat based at Sovereign Harbour. She is virtually unsinkable and self-righting. It is a sobering thought that the Eastbourne Lifeboat Men have saved over 700 lives since the service was first launched (two years before the RNLI was established) in 1822, and rescued countless thousands more. The RNLI is still funded by voluntary contributions.

Some of the Chester fishermen on Eastbourne beach, taken after WW2 about 1948, left to right Andrew William Chester, Roy Chester, Andrew Basil Chester, and finally granddad, Andrew Chester. Andrew Basil's wife, (whom he met at a dance at the Fisherman's Club and still lives along Royal Parade, opposite the fishing sheds), took the picture on her box brownie. Andrew Chester was the last of the fishermen who used to chase the shoals of herring and mackerel all along the Channel in the time-honoured way.
The boat was the Olive Joyce.

The Chester family next to their boat the Olive Joyce. Eastbourne Beach circa

Bob Page's old fish shop is currently the Southern Head Fishing Company. You can buy fresh fish there straight from the Eastbourne boats. Next to the fish shop is the Allchorn huts where the last two old pleasure boats are housed. There are steps underway to renovate the old Allchorn Pleasure Boats to once more take visitors on trips around Beachy Head Lighthouse. Lloyd Stebbings (a fiberglass expert) is putting in a huge effort to get at least one of the boats seaworthy.

Fisherman's Green is still the thriving hub of the Eastbourne's shore based fishermen. Many of the boats are run by the old Eastbourne fishing families. Most of the other local working boats (not on the beach) usually come out of Sovereign Harbour. As tourism boomed the first Eastbourne Pleasure Boats were started. William Allchorn first supplemented his fishing with his summer pleasure boats in 1861. By 1910 there were dozens of pleasure boats. By the 1970's there were just two pleasure boats left along the promenade, the Southern Queen and the William Allchorn.

The William Allchorn was purpose made pleasure boat. It was built in 1950 from Government funds, put aside by the Ministry of Defence as payment for the loss of the Enchantress during evacuations at Dunkirk. William 'Booner' Wood would often

skipper the boat around Beachy Head. He regularly parked his Triumph motorcycle along the seafront, near the boat winches. Brian Allchorn put the boats up for sale in 1994.

Sometime after the Millennium, around 2007, they were removed from service due to new safety rules and maintenance. When in service they were moved daily from their berth at Fisherman's Green to their tourist pick-up point just west of Eastbourne Pier. On calm nights they berthed at sea. A World War Two amphibious craft (known as a 'Duck' after its DUKW abbreviation) would lay out the tourists boarding planks that led from the beach to the craft. As kids it was great fun, when the weather was rough, to watch fat holiday makers (we called them grockles) trying to get along the bouncing planks while clinging for dear life to the hand rails. We never saw anyone fall in, but were ever hopeful! Photo Geoffrey Barry.

This is one of the Allchorn pleasure boats, taken in May of 2019. A sad sight, slowly perishing on the beach at Fisherman's Green. Out of the water you can clearly see her size. It once carried up to 100 passengers along the coast. With a full load she sat so low in the water it was easy to drop your hand over the side into the sea. As you can see she has a beautiful shallow clinker hull. When the tide was high enough the boats would actually sail between the cliff face and the Beachy Head lighthouse. In the foreground are the giant wheels that once carried her in and out of the sea. At one time nearly 120 licences were regularly issued for pleasure boats along Eastbourne seafront. Today there are none.

CHAPTER 15

From 1900 most of the Eastbourne fishing families were all in one place, east of the Redoubt Fortress. Here they continued to flourish. Markets started daily at 7.00am by the fishing huts. Around two dozen fish sellers or 'hawkers' would buy the catch, load it onto their flat barrows and walk the streets of Eastbourne selling fresh fish.

The same method was used right up until the 1970's. We often bought fish from Bob Clark's barrow. Bob's brother ran the local tackle shop and Bob sold fish from his barrow. Bob, as he often told me, had the unusual distinction of being at my birth. Well almost! One hot day in July of 1957 my mum was buying fish from Bob, outside number 22 Eversfield Road. Without warning she suddenly went into labour. Bob, in panic, hot-tailed it up the road as fast as his short legs could push his barrow! Mum shuffled inside to have me on the couch. He would always laugh, saying that he had known me since I was a baby!

Fishing in Eastbourne peaked just before the outbreak of the First World War. After the war things were never the same as many of the families suffered the loss of the young blood that would have naturally taken over their trades. A government grant helped the surviving fishermen to rebuild some of their equipment. It helped, but from the1920's a slow downward spiral took place, especially when more advanced commercial-ised techniques (from the larger harbours along the coast) slowly outpaced the old traditional methods.

Out of all the old fishermen's tales from that period, none is more amazing than that of 'Old Mug' Huggett and his wife Louisa. They had fallen on hard times after being evicted from their lodgings. Both were in their 70's when they decided to live rough on the beach, by the fishing station. For years they would stack fish boxes and crates up to make a rough dwelling, stretching out oiled canvas for a roof. They washed and hung out their clothes between the fishing boats and lived on handouts from the other fishermen, cooking their food on open fires. Both were considered eccentric and seemed to enjoy the wild life they lived. For years, 'Old Mug' and his wife beachcombed for scraps, repaired nets, and eked a living on the beach.

Many fishermen subsidised their income by turning to the pleasure boating industry that flourished in the summertime as Eastbourne became a premier tourist resort. Rowing boats were used to take holidaymakers out on the water and small sailing boats took the more adventurous further out to sea. Larger pleasure boats could take tourists all the way to Seaford and back.

Nothing was stopping the Duke's new boomtown. Now Eastbourne, with its excellent new rail links from the capital and ample building land, was becoming the perfect seaside resort for wealthy tourists and those wishing to escape the grime of the big cities. A Summer capital for polite society, all built around the health-giving, purifying sea air and refreshing waters.

Doctors in the smog-filled cities started to praise the virtues of a rest by the seaside, often prescribing a week in the sea air to restore normal bodily functions. Some even went as far as to suggest drinking the seawater! I bet that didn't last long. I can't imagine a better way to make you feel instantly ill.

In 1772 workers discovered the foundations of a Roman villa along the promenade and legend tells that mosaics are still beneath the Carpet Gardens, though recent excavation in 2018 failed to discover any. Apparently locals say that they need to look beneath the old fountain!

The 125 bedroom Queens Hotel was completed in 1880 and opened in June of that year. Henry Currey's superb hotel was built on the site of Field House and its meadow.

The seaward area in front of the Queens Hotel was once known as Splash Point due to the huge waves that crashed into the sea wall there. However after the sea wall was extended to the Redoubt Fortress, Splash Point naturally moved there as well. In recent years, due to the heavy shingle built up at Splash Point, you rarely get the bone-shuddering waves crashing onto the promenade and the spectacular plumes of water that followed. It is said that The Queens Hotel's size and height was to block all views eastward from the promenade (to protect visitors from the locals, lower classes, and fishermen).

The magnificent Chatsworth Hotel was opened to visitors in 1905. It is a perfect example of Edwardian architecture in the 'grand style' and must be one of the finest Edwardian hotels in the world. It was family run for decades but in the past few years we have seen its sale and closure. Since its last sale it has been undergoing extensive renovations and restorations. It is hoped that 2019 will see it open once more.

The 8th Duke of Devonshire, Spencer Compton Cavendish, loved Eastbourne and his earliest memories were fond ones. "I remember visiting Compton Place with my father. As a child I would walk from Compton Place to the Wish Tower by a footpath through fields of waving corn, through an expanse of land which is now occupied by well-ordered streets and prosperous residences."

The Cavendish Hotel on the corner of Devonshire Place was named after William Cavendish the 7th Duke of Devonshire (1808-1891). Situated on the seafront with majestic views and only a few minutes from the railway station, it was the ideal building to attract a wealth of new visitors to the expanding town. The hotel's architect was Thomas. E. Knightley. It was built the same year that the Devonshire Park and Baths Company was formed in 1873. The hotel was extended in 1891.

This is the Cavendish in 2017, still looking resplendent in the winter sunshine. You will notice the east side of the hotel is very different to its original design.

The Cavendish Hotel on 4 May 1942 after nine German Messerschmitt Me109 dropped their 250kg high-explosive bombs on Eastbourne. The Duke, 'That finest flower of Victorian nobility' as one paper reported, 'sits unmoved by the whole affair.' Picture courtesy of David Arscott, Gordon Clark.

In its long history, the Cavendish Hotel has witnessed all the great changes to our town. I was told that when the hotel first opened it only had eight toilets for over 200 rooms! That might seem crazy but that was still two more than The Grand Hotel! How times have changed. Interestingly it was under the 7th Duke's insistence that there should be no shops along the seafront. It was his dream of a resort built by 'gentlemen for gentlemen' that produced the elegance that we still see today along the promenade. Eastbourne did truly become the empress of watering places.

The statue of the 7th Duke of Devonshire now sits at the head of Devonshire Place, between the Cumberland and the Cavendish hotels. It was hotels like these that the Duke had dreamed of creating to attract tourism, the latest craze in 19th century Britain. The Dukes statue gazes seaward. To his back is the superb 80ft wide boulevard leading to the centre of the seaside town that he visualised. Due to his foresight and determination there will be a corner of Sussex that is forever Devonshire.

Out of all the statues in Eastbourne, one of the most interesting is that to The Royal Sussex Regiment, right next to Eastbourne Pier. The statue is of a soldier in full uniform from the Bengal Regiment of the East India Company (which eventually became the 2nd Battalion of The Royal Sussex Regiment). The plaques list the early actions abroad and the loyal servicemen who gave their lives on tours and in campaigns.

The unveiling, on a chilly February day in 1906, attracted so many spectators that special trains had to be laid on. The unveiling of the statue was by the Duke of Norfolk (a major in the 2nd Battalion of the Royal Sussex Regiment himself). He was accompanied by a Guard of Honour from the Royal Sussex Regiment and many other dignitaries, including the Mayor of Eastbourne.

143

CHAPTER 16

DEVONSHIRE BATHS

No book on Eastbourne would be complete without a mention of some of its most impressive buildings. They are long gone now but in their heyday the Devonshire Baths was the finest indoor bathing facility in Britain.

The pinnacle of the Duke's dream for Eastbourne as an Empress of Watering Places came true with the building of The Devonshire Baths in Carlisle Road. Once again, George Ambrose Wallis was the designer and the baths were built by local contractor, James Peerless. His workmen undertook one of the most impressive building projects in Victorian Britain. It meant that Eastbourne would have the finest baths in the country.

The baths were built to resemble Turkish Baths with a massive 80ft Lombardo-Venetian tower, holding three huge water tanks (and hiding the chimney from the boilers). The tower's water tanks were to supply the baths that were on the ground level. These would prove to be extremely popular with people who would walk in off the street, straight into a hot bath for sixpence. The local houses and hotels also made use of the hot water, which could be delivered to reception for a penny a bucket.

The baths were opened on April Fool's Day 1874. With the Duke a major shareholder in the newly formed Devonshire Park & Baths Company, the baths became a great draw and crowd pleaser.

These 'state of the art' pools were an amazing example of brilliant 19th Century engineering. They were sunk well below the high water mark so that they could easily be filled from the sea. You could bathe in the 'healing' salt water baths or swim in the desalinated pools, all carefully segregated of course! Devonshire Baths had the biggest heated saltwater pools in the country, the largest being 166ft long. No expense was spared and each changing cubicle came complete with a chamber pot! Water was pumped from the sea with the tides twice daily.

By 1923 the Devonshire Baths were purchased by the town (who had been after them since the late Victorian Times). They were used for generations by the public and schools alike. It was a sad day when storms damaged the seawater supply pipes so badly that the council (to save money) decided to stop using sea water. This started a downward slide that coincided with poor tourism in the early 1970's. The fantastic tower was demolished first in 1973. The baths closed in 1977.

The usual Council under funding had led to the final nail in the coffin for one of the finest Victorian baths in the country. They lay derelict for years before finally being demolished in 1999. Later development of the site was a nightmare as the baths had been sunk deep into the ground, leaving an enormous hole to be filled before any building could start.

Interestingly, one of my first jobs after leaving college was working (for a brief period) for Eastbourne Council as an engineer. One of my duties was to inspect the derelict buildings at Devonshire Baths and make sure that the pumps were working (they kept the lower levels from flooding). It was so depressing to see the magnificent structure I grew up with being left to rot. There were two massive 20 ton Lancashire boilers, semi-submerged in filthy oily water. It was these boilers that once not only supplied the heating for the pools and baths but piped hot water and steam under the roads to heat the Winter Garden.

CHAPTER 17
EASTBOURNE PIER

Eastbourne's most prominent feature along the seafront, visited by millions, is its superb pier. It was one of the Duke's best ideas and one of the finest landmarks in the town. Some say it is the best surviving example of its type in the world.

The idea was simple, the perfect focal point to draw visitors out from their hotels so that they could venture along his new parade. His 'Grand Parade' ran from the pier to his pleasure grounds at Devonshire Park.

The proposal for a pier was first put to an eager Duke around 1863. The idea of visitors 'walking on water' appealed to him. By the spring of 1865 the Eastbourne Pier Company was formed and a design from superb pier builder Eugenius Birch was finally selected. Birch was a designer, architect and builder, from bridges and viaducts in India, to docks and harbours down the west of England. His great masterstroke was his stunning piers. You can almost see the Indian influence in his design for Eastbourne pier. At sunrise it often looks like far-off pavilions.

The first pile of Eastbourne Pier was screwed into the seabed on 18th April 1866. In a stroke of engineering genius, the pier struts, pylons or piles had screw blades attached to the bottom end and were actually screwed down into the seabed by specially designed equipment. It allowed the pier to survive most storms and even a few World Wars. Many say that Eastbourne Pier, the seventh pier of the 14 designed by Birch, was his finest. Only a handful of his piers still survive, some in terrible condition.

The pier was once again a masterpiece of Victorian engineering and the first stage of the 1000 foot pier was officially opened with much pomp and ceremony on 13th June 1870, by Lord Edward Cavendish (son of the 7th Duke). It was noted that almost every person in the area who could get to Eastbourne Seafront on that day was present.

However, work was weather dependent, and was way behind schedule. It was not completed for another two years and even then many improvements followed. The original pier was flat and much plainer with no stalls or merchandise for sale (as per the Duke's wishes).

At the beginning of 1887 a great storm erupted and damaged a huge part of the foundations at the land end of the pier. It was rebuilt with stronger deeper supports. It explains the sloping deck halfway along, that suddenly drops to the next level. As tourism boomed, in 1888 (the same year Jack the Ripper was stalking London), a massive 400 seater pavilion was con-structed for shows. It was a busy season as people escaped the city in droves for some light relief by the seaside.

In 1893, a better lower landing stage was built on the end. This allowed larger paddle steamers and ships to berth. The Waverly was still a regular visitor every summer when I was young, and often took holidaymakers back to London. Seven years later an even bigger 1000 seat theatre and bar replaced the original. Part of the construction included the wonderful Camera Obscura. As a child it was always a treat to see the panoramic sea views and hotels projected onto the mirrored surface of the obscura. When the mirror cracked it was replaced with a painted surface. It worked but was a poor substitute. More amusements and arcades were slowly added, including a small bandstand and huge ballroom. The sprung floor ballroom, decorated mainly in subtle blues, became known as The Blue Room.

In 1940, during the Second World War, a large chunk of the decking was removed and a section of the pier dismantled. It was basically cut in two. This was to stop enemy boats using the pier as a landing platform. Anti-aircraft and machine guns were installed to guard against invasion. The servicemen would go out to their positions on the pier by boat. In 1942 the structure was damaged by an exploding mine, which was probably one of the Allied ones that had come adrift in stormy weather.

When dancing faded away, in the austere post-war 1950's, the wonderful ballroom was converted into an amusement arcade. In 1968 Trust House Forte bought the pier and carried on investing in its upkeep. Fishing was allowed along both sides and end. Small cubicles along each side were crammed with fortune tellers, sweet sellers, and bits of seaside paraphernalia. My favourite were the glass workers. They created little glass souvenirs in front of your eyes, with gas torches and mesmerising skill.

In the 1970's investment in the pier declined and like so many other piers, it slowly rotted away. It was still open to the public but many of the stalls and shops had closed. It became home to more pigeons and starlings than tourists. The starlings miraculous antics above the pier became an attraction in their own right. On some evenings countless thousands of starlings created airborne acrobatics with their mesmerising murmurations, before dropping to roost on the steel structure beneath the pier at nightfall. Most were eventually frightened off with constant explosions and artificial screeching bird noises by the pier owners who were not wildlife friendly.

The theatre was hardly being used when in January of 1970 it was destroyed in a fire. The main attraction after that was the nightclub Dixieland which became Atlantis. In 1985 a massive injection of money saw the pier resurrected with new arcades and shops.

The Great Storm of 1987 damaged the landing stages at the far end. No more ships could dock for passengers. No investment was forthcoming to repair the damage. This was a bonus for the fishermen as fishing had been banned from both sides of the pier. From that time on the sea end of the pier became exclusively the haunt of the fishermen, bass being the prime target as they fed around the pylons and mackerel shoals in the summer as they passed by.

In 1990 another big investment saw the building of a new entrance to the pier costing over half a million pounds. It was opened by The 11th Duke of Devonshire on 15 June 1991.

In 2009, Eastbourne Pier was upgraded to a Grade II listing. Interestingly, the only Grade I pier in the country is at Clevedon in Somerset. The great news with the listing is that it brought Eastbourne Pier into a special catalogue of important buildings needing extreme effort to protect and preserve them. Later that year it was put up for sale for £5·5 million. There were no takers.

After a long dry summer, on 30 July 2014 an electrical fire in the Blue Room Amusement Arcade broke out. With the strong westerly winds it soon became out of control and due to the receding tide the fire hoses from the boats were unable to reach the Blue Room. Little could be done as the lead-domed ballroom burnt. About one third of the pier was destroyed before the fire was brought under control. It became worldwide news. Even the Prime Minister of the time, David Cameron, rushed down to have his photo taken by the wreckage. Within a few months of the fire the damaged structures were quickly removed and the pier was made safe for visitors. Interestingly metal 'detectorists', who had regularly scoured the shingle below the pier found their hobby incredibly frustrating, because countless metal particles from the burnt pier fell onto the beach.

Although rumours abounded about it being arson, no evidence was found and in 2015 the police closed their files on the fire. That same year, hotel impresario Sheik Abid Gulzar bought the pier for an undisclosed sum. In the poor state it was, from fire damage, years of neglect, and lack of investment, it needed someone with will and determination to bring it back from the brink of destruction.

Sheik Abid Gulzar was that man, investing heavily, bringing what's left of the magnificent pier back into order. His team of dedicated workmen have undertaken a program of improvements and even picked out the domes in gold. Some of the lights where the Blue Room once stood have been left fire-damaged as a reminder of that terrible fire.

Eastbourne Pier, known to locals now as 'the Sheikspier' is still considered one of the finest examples of a 19th century seaside pier. Some of the wooden floor is still laid out how the original Duke wanted (with gaps). When you look down as you walk at the right speed it still gives the impression that you are actually walking on water!

A storm erupted at the beginning of 1887. It destroyed a large part of the original pier. Stronger foundations were added with a taller promenade. It explains the drop to the seaward section of the pier today. It is interesting to note that 100 years later another Great Storm hit Eastbourne in 1987.

The fishing ban on Eastbourne Pier upset many locals but there are rumours that Sheik Abid Gulzar is softening his stance and may allow limited fishing, on the end only.

Eastbourne Pier was the biggest tourist attraction on the seafront and drew millions of visitors. This picture taken around the First World War Era shows rows of cars picking up tourists for outings around the area. The Pier is still a centre for bus and coach trips.

Eastbourne Pier had its own small bandstand where music was played every weekend and most days during the main holiday season. Where the Pavilion Tea Rooms stand today was another popular bandstand.

153

After a lower landing platform was added, steamships could pick up passengers at most times except the lowest tides. Some trips went all the way to London. The Waverly was still stopping regularly at Eastbourne when I was younger but storm damage to the landing platforms brought an end to that.

Eastbourne Pier held the envious position as one of the finest piers in Europe before the 2014 fire. In the early morning the silhouette of the structure looks like some far pavilions. I wonder if that was what the designer Eugenius Birch was trying to achieve after his journeys in India.

I took this photo just before the disastrous fire in the summer of 2014. Shortly after this photo the Amazing Blue Room would be lost forever.

From my window in Willingdon I saw the smoke stretching all the way to Hastings. I rushed down to see the last part of the Blue Room fall into the sea. The police were clearing the promenade in case the wind changed. It was a sad day to see all those priceless memories disappear forever.

Luckily the national impact of the devastating fire urged David Cameron, the Prime Minister at the time, to promise swift action. Indeed within weeks the damaged structure was carefully dismantled to allow workmen onto the parts that could be saved. The only sign of the fire today is the burnt out lights which once surrounded the Blue Room.

Even with the beautiful Blue Room missing, Eastbourne Pier can still be counted amongst the finest examples of Eugenius Birch's work.

The last image of the fabulous Blue Room, lost on that hot July afternoon in 2014.

157

CHAPTER 18
THE BANDSTAND

As the Duke's dream of a booming seaside town became a reality, entertainment along his promenade was proving more and more popular, from Punch & Judy shows to donkey rides. Eastbourne was settling into a gentle seaside resort, attracting a more sedate type of family, leaving the other booming seaside towns on the South Coast, like Brighton and Hastings to cater for the more adventurous and excitable crowds.

Constant improvements were taking place and in 1893 the first bandstand was built along the promenade. It was the traditional 'birdcage' style that had been built in towns and parks across the country. The entertainment proved so popular that by 1899 a municipal Eastbourne orchestra was formed to play regularly there.

It was at this bandstand that local bandsman, John Wesley Woodward played. He was one of the musicians on the RMS Titanic that sank on 15 April 1912. Legend tells that the 32 year old musician, along with his other band members, carried on playing as the RMS Titanic sunk. Band leader, 34 year old Wallace Henry Hartley led his eight member band, keeping the passengers calm as they climbed into the lifeboats. John was one of the 1,503 people who died on that fateful trip. His body was never identified. A commemorative plaque to John is on the later bandstand that we have today.

In 1934, as part of the massive new seafront improvements, the decision was made to build a bigger and better bandstand. This would allow larger bands and bigger crowds. The plans were to encompass viewing decks and an upper colonnade. Luckily for Eastbourne, local Borough Council engineer, Leslie Rosevere, had ideas that proved far better than anyone else could provide. As Borough Engineer he would normally have been responsible for road layouts, flood precautions and local services, but he also became heavily involved with the new seafront improvements that were underway at the time. He put forward a stunning neo-Grecian circular design on a grand scale with hardly a straight line in sight. The upper level would be supported on Greek style Corinthian pillars, giving the structure an open airy feel. Sliding doors would allow access and views from nearly all sides with a protective barrier wall facing the sea.

The new bandstand would be built right on the edge of the sea. It meant that at high tides, half the construction could be in the water. The sea-facing base would be curved upwards so that the rolling waves would crash into her seawall, be thrown up, and then back into the sea in spectacular fashion. This is difficult to imagine today as the high artificial beach has stopped all but the very highest tides even reaching the Bandstand. Certainly the brilliant design of the base is currently wasted. However, if the seafront was to return to its natural state, without the false shingle beach, spectacular waves would once again crash into the bandstand's curving foundations.

Before the artificial beach it was a favourite fishing haunt for many (including me). We had the protection of the upper promenade above, and the benefit of casting the bait easily from the lower promenade into the sea. It was even lit at night.

By 1935 the stunning blue-domed roof was complete. With its yellow biscuit cream tile façade and beautiful sky blue tiled roof it looked like a flying saucer. It was topped with a spire made of a new-fangled non-rusting metal called stainless steel. Nearly all the materials had to be specially made for Rosevere's amazing design. There is no other bandstand like Eastbourne's. It is still unique. The bandstand itself cost a staggering £28,765 at its completion (well up on its estimate).

The first concerts were held in July of 1935. Three were planned for the day. It was a huge success with thousands crowding in to see the bands play. It was officially opened on 5 August 1935 by the Lord Lieutenant of Sussex, The Rt Hon Lord Leconfield G.C.V.O. The mayor at the time was woman councillor Miss Thornton J.P. By her side was Chairman of the Committee that approved Rosevere's design, Alderman Lt. Col. Roland Gwynne D.S.O., D.L., J.P.

Bands and groups have been playing there regularly ever since, the most popular day (weather depending) always being the Boxing Day Special. Today it is advertised as the busiest bandstand in the country.

The early 'Birdcage' bandstand was replaced by the stunning bandstand that we see today. If you get a chance, look at the base of the Bandstand and see Leslie Rosevere's stunning engineering design that would sweep the incoming waves back out to sea. Also note how every tile had to be specially made for this unique structure.

Eastbourne bandstand is the busiest in the country with a series of events held throughout the year. Its brilliant design, by Eastbourne Borough Council engineer, Leslie Rosevere, is a masterpiece that has withstood the worst elements for decades. Notice on the low outer sea-edge of the semi-circular promenade the curving sea wall is just visible. Before the adding of an artificial beach you could see the full height and design of the spectacular design that threw the incoming waves back out to sea. It was great fun on wild days watching the rollers come crashing into the Bandstand.

CHAPTER 19
THE LIFEBOAT MUSEUM

Out of all the seafront properties, none has a more fascinating story than that of the Lifeboat Museum. It was originally intended as a lifeboat station. From 1899, for the first few years of its life, the William Terriss Life Boat House was home to the James Stevens No 6 Lifeboat. But before we explore the strange and gruesome tale of how the building came into being, let me set the scene of a murder that shocked Victorian England and how Eastbourne ended up with a lifeboat station in the wrong place!

William Terriss was a theatre actor and the superstar of his day. Long before radio and television, film and mass media, the theatres ruled supreme. Theatre stars were the biggest names in the papers besides the 'Royals'. In late Victorian England, no name was greater than that of the handsome ever-young actor William Terriss. His life burnt bright but was tragically and brutally cut short. Scotsman, William Charles James Lewin, took the stage name William Terriss when he decided that it would be an actor's life for him. He quickly rose to prominence with stunning performances from Henry VIII to Romeo in Romeo & Juliet. By his late 40's Terriss was in his prime and the most exalted actor on the London stage. The ever-youthful looking actor played the hero on stage and in real life after surviving being shipwrecked at sea. In 1885, as a keen sailor himself (serving on a Merchant navy tea clippers) he rescued a young lad from drowning and was awarded a medal. The world-wise sailor turned actor even had a daughter born on Stanley in the Falkland Islands (more of Mary Ellaline Lewin shortly). This made the actor's star shine even brighter and his shows became sell out performances. Being the biggest box office draw of the time, theatre owners and impresarios flocked to him with offers. He was the A-lister of the day, specialising in melodramas and Shakespearian tragedies.

Terriss was appearing at the Royal Adelphi Theatre in the Strand, London. A new play called Harbour Lights was going down a storm and one Winter's night in December of 1897 the theatre was packed for the start of the show. However, lurking in the shadows at the back of the theatre was one very jealous and dangerous young man, Dicky Prince. Richard Archer Prince was the polar opposite to Terriss. He was a failed actor who felt cheated. He constantly badgered Terriss for bit parts. Terriss took Prince in, helped and supported him, but it was never enough. Prince grew darker and darker, making Terriss the sole object of hatred for his own failings. Terriss was the centre of every party while Prince was left searching for scraps.

On 16 December 1897 Prince was stalking the shadows, waiting for Terriss on the back steps of the Adelphi. As Terriss arrived to prepare for his show, Prince stepped out of the darkness and plunged a short knife into his back. As the shocked Terriss turned he struck again, plunging the knife into his side. Then as Terriss was facing him he struck the fateful final blow, straight into his heart. For a second Terriss recognised the young man that he had done so much to help. Prince pulled free and tried to run. The scuffle was seen and passersby grabbed Prince, ripping off his heavy coat to expose the young actor before pinning him to the ground.

Terriss lay dying as his leading lady, Jessie Millward, pushed through the crowd and let out a terrible gasp. She adored her leading man and clutched the dying actor to her breast. He was bleeding profusely. Covered in his blood she called to the crowd for silence so that she could hear Terriss, who was trying to speak. As he gasped for breath legend tells that he whispered to her that he would return. He then slumped in her arms with the final words, "Oh God." The greatest actor of the age had been murdered.

At 7.22pm, while theatre goers waited patiently at the front of the theatre for the show to start, Terriss, just 50, lay dead at the back. One of the stage crew had to go on stage and announce to the shocked audience what had just happened. Several women collapsed as the theatre was cleared and the police arrived. It was a tragic scene that had jumped from the stage (and one of Terriss's melodramas) straight into real life.

Late editions of the London Papers carried the news to a shocked capital. He was so well known it was as if a friend had died. His funeral at Brompton Cemetery was the largest ever seen, with over 10,000 people trying to cram in. His coffin nearly fell as it was buffeted by eager mourners. *The Daily Telegraph*, who had often covered his plays, started a Memorial Fund in his name. Even as Prince came to trial more money poured in. Strangest of all was that Terriss's understudy, Frederick Lane, had a premonition of Terriss' death the day before he was murdered. It is said that at exactly the same time he was stabbed, Lane's dog became uncontrollable, scaring the entire household with his howling!

Prince's trial was a farce. Destined for the gallows for a cold blooded premeditated murder, his defence cleverly twisted the case into one of insanity. Prince acted out his part impeccably, twitching and stuttering like a lunatic. At the back of the court was Terriss's 26 year old daughter Ellaline Lewin, quietly watching proceedings. A popular actress herself, she had also used Terriss as her stage name and had apparently spent time in Eastbourne convalescing when she was younger.

Prince was found to be insane and sentenced to life in Broadmoor Criminal Lunatic Asylum, where he died in 1936. It caused an outrage at the time with actors and writers filling the pages of the daily periodicals with their disgust. However all this publicity added to the coffers of the ever growing Memorial Fund for Terriss. Many say that Terriss' last words were prophetic as his ghost is said to haunt the Covent Garden theatre area to this day. Though the papers claimed Terriss was 48 years old his grave is clearly marked 50.

The Daily Telegraph decided that the money raised would be perfect for a lifeboat station for the Royal Life Boat Institution. Eastbourne was chosen, as the seaside town had been a favourite haunt of Terriss, when he had time to spare. At a cost of £1,314 work was completed in 1898. On 16 July 1898 the William Terriss Memorial Lifeboat House was opened in

Eastbourne by Her Grace the Duchess of Devonshire. If ever you are down that way the large plaque on the side of the museum makes for interesting reading.

Terriss's lifeboat station was not really practical. In stormy weather the largest waves hit the shore directly opposite the station, making it almost impossible to launch. This proved so troublesome that the lifeboat station was moved along to Marine Parade, and eventually to Fisherman's Green where the inshore lifeboat is still housed today; the main lifeboat now being berthed at Sovereign Harbour.

Rather than waste the superb building, the RLNI used the boathouse to house the redundant James Stevens lifeboat as a tourist attraction. This proved so popular that the RLNI decided to open their first museum. On 22 March 1937 the William Terriss Boat House became the first ever RNLI museum, and it was opened with much pomp and ceremony by Sir Godfrey Baring Bt (Chairman of the RLNI). Attending was Ellaline Terriss who had become Lady Ellaline Hicks. The distinct clock above the station was added in commemoration of the coronation of King George VI the same year.

William's daughter, Ellaline, had gone on to have a successful career on the stage. She later made the transition to silent movies, then 'talkies'. After a fruitful career, Ellaline did her last film in 1939 called The Four Just Men. As World War Two raged, in 1940 she did a final tour with The Entertainments National Service Association (ENSA), to entertain British troops in the Middle East. After she returned she retired.

In 1962, the TV personality Eamonn Andrews, surprised her as she painted quietly in her back garden and she starred in his program, This Is Your Life. Ellaline, who had witnessed such tragedy in her life, with her father being murdered, her mother dying shortly after, and outliving her husband, went on to live to the ripe old age of 100. She died at the Holy Family Nursing Home in London on 16 June 1971. And so ends a fascinating journey.

Interestingly, the Lifeboat Museum is the only property along the entire seafront that is allowed to sell merchandise. In line with the original Duke's wishes, no shops of any kind were permissible, but the Lifeboat Museum is allowed a little leeway because of its charity status.

The William Terriss Memorial Lifeboat House was built with funds raised from the murder of William Terriss on 16 December 1897. William Terriss was one of the foremost actors of his age and his death shocked a nation. Funds poured in for his memorial.

Often, the only way to spot a vessel in distress was to keep a keen eye on the horizon. Here is James Levoir doing just that, opposite the Lifeboat Station in the 1920's. Sue Huggett Collection.

The James Stevens No 6 was the first lifeboat to be housed at the station. It arrived in 1899, the year after the station was officially opened by Her Grace the Duchess of Devonshire (on the afternoon of the 16 July 1898). In 1924 the James Stevens had finished service as a working boat. It was decided to house it permanently at what was then the William Terriss Boat House. The boat and boathouse attracted many visitors, becoming a firm attraction along the Eastbourne Seafront. In 1937 the boathouse became the first ever RNLI Lifeboat Museum (with the James Stevens on proud display). William Terriss' daughter, Lady Ellaline Hicks, was present at the opening by Sir Godfrey Baring Bt (chairman of the RNLI).

Lifeboat Flag Day was usually around late summer and often coincided with royal visits and big fundraising events. Displays stretched all the way along the promenade from the old Lifeboat Station to Fisherman's Green (where the lifeboat was housed before moving to Sovereign Harbour). The fishermen, who turned to tourism during the busy summer months, often berthed their smaller pleasure craft on the beach opposite The Albion Hotel. In this picture, possibly from July 1931 (and the Royal visit by The Prince of Wales), you can see the oars used in the structure. The boatmen are proudly wearing their medals won during rescue missions at sea. Sue Huggett Collection.

During his summer visit in June and July of 1931, the future King, the Prince of Wales, attended several events in town. He planted an oak tree at Gilbert's Recreation Ground (once the old Crumbles Pond that is now Princes Park). He visited the new slipway for the lifeboat at Fisherman's Green and watched the lifeboat launch, and here he is meeting some of the boat-men. Note their medals. Sue Huggett Collection.

This is the Jane Holland beaching at Fisherman's Green. The Jane Holland has to be one of Eastbourne's most fascinating lifeboats. Originally built by J Samuel White, she entered service at Eastbourne in 1929. No one had any idea what a little survivor she would be (boats are usually female as they look after the men on board). Six months into World War Two the British expeditionary Force were cornered on the beaches at Dunkirk. Hundreds of thousands of troops were pinned down by the advancing Nazi Forces. Large ships could not get close enough for evacuation so the word secretly went out to all the small ships across the land. Operation Dynamo swung into action as the call was answered by fishermen, lifeboatmen, retired sailors and almost anyone who was heroic enough to volunteer. The Jane Holland was the oldest of the 19 lifeboats that took part in the evacuation.

Over a few days between 26 May and 4 June around 338,000 men were rescued by Dunkirk's 'little ships'. Operation Dynamo became known as the 'Miracle of Dunkirk' and saved Britain at its most perilous time. The Jane Holland was strafed by enemy aircraft, hit by a British motor torpedo boat, hit by a French vessel and abandoned. The French then tried to blow her out of the water as she had become a floating hazard. However the little lifeboat proved to be made of tough stuff. She was later spotted, still afloat and drifting, with over 500 bullet holes and shrapnel holes in her. Astoundingly she was repaired and put back into service at Eastbourne. She served until the early 1950's before being placed in reserve. Eventually she was sold and possibly renamed 'The Reporter'. She was last spotted off Birkenhead. If her history is anything to go by she is probably moored up somewhere, still afloat! Sue Huggett Collection.

CHAPTER 20
THE ITALIAN GARDENS

Now that we have dealt with some of the more interesting buildings along the Duke's seafront, let's step back a little and continue with our walking tour at Holywell. From the Sugar Loaf we move down the precarious cliff path, making our way to the steps, which drop steeply down to the beach. Be careful here and take your time to stop and look at the amazing views. Depending on the tides you can sometimes get a great view of the two reefs and the lagoon between them.

Once down on the beach (which regularly tops the Marine Conservation Society Good Beach Guide) we turn east towards the town. After clambering over the first wooden groyne we come across the last remaining water source pouring out of the rock face – Holywell itself. There is usually a sign there but it gets nicked regularly, vandalised, or just swept away by the high tides. It was the remains of this well that was blessed in 2010.

Our early ancestors assumed that the gifts of life could only have come from their gods, so it was naturally assumed that pure water gushing forth from the earth was a gift from above. I have been told that the reason the water is so pure is that some of the water originates from ancient melted glacial waters, stored millennia ago deep within the cliffs. The water is forced up by a geological fault between the chalk, greensand and gault clay, mixing with rain water filtering down through the chalk. In reality, though packed with minerals that many believe are beneficial, what made Holywell water so special was not what the water had in it but what it did not! It was almost pollutant free.

When I was a kid, water poured out from several places along the cliff base but in the last 50 years only one small area has remained constant. Much of the time the well is hidden by heavy shingle pushed up from rough seas. Sometimes it stinks! So it's not all good news. Seaweed thrown in on stormy days rots at the base of the cliffs until it is either swept away or dries and is blown away. However, pull the weed away, move a few stones and as if by magic the spring water is there. Crystal clear and sweet, and legend tells, blessed with healing powers. Though I have to admit it didn't cure my old dog's stinky skin, even after several savage washes!

After leaving the well we walk along the beach towards Eastbourne. Look up at the white cliff face; you are looking at the sight that sailors first saw when approaching our island home. They named the huge cliffs 'the white place', translated from ancient Greek it became Albion. Albion is still the oldest name associated with our country.

Within a few minutes you come across the bathing huts where King George V and Queen Mary changed for a dip in 1935. Better still the Holywell Café for a bite to eat. You have to wonder if King George had a chalet there by accident or was it to be close to the healing water of Holywell. It may have just been a coincidence, but it is well known that King George tried many things to regain his frail health. It is said that several famous people, including Charles Dickens and T E Lawrence sipped from the waters. Some people dispute that Charles Dickens ever visited Eastbourne but others say he was a regular visitor, with tearooms being named after him and plaques put up where he stayed in Old Town. Some say he even put on plays at the Lamb Inn, opposite where he stayed. As your tour guide I am aware that I am waffling off-topic again, so let's get on. The Holywell Café (better known by the Meads residents as The Holywell Tea Chalet) was finished in 1921, cleverly using labour from the unemployed workers around the town.

While you are walking, notice the sea kale and other rare seaside plants, some once eaten by our ancestors. Also the multitude of different stones and pebbles that crunch beneath your feet as you walk along. Some of these stones are field flints that have fallen from the eroding chalk face, some are just bits of old brick, glass, concrete or pottery from our industrial heritage, but some have rolled across the seabeds of the world to be heaved up onto our shoreline. A few would even have been blown out of volcanoes as lava. If you rub two of these (usually deep grey) together, you can smell the burning sulphur from the centre of our planet. Wherever these beautiful multi-coloured pebbles originated from, all their jagged edges have been polished smooth by time and the ever moving tides.

From the beach we start to move upward by Holywell tea chalet to the Italian Gardens. This huge cutting in the chalk hillside was once the busy Gore Chalk Pit that I mentioned earlier. Its chalk was used for many of the foundations of the grand houses and hotels of Eastbourne. Rather interestingly, when work in the original pit was found to be polluting the water from Holywell, all work in the pit was stopped. I have to wonder if that was one of the deciding reasons that the powers that be wanted the fishermen off the old land at Holywell as well.

If you think about it, their pollution would have been directly above the water supplies. So if Gore Chalk Pit was polluting the water, a quarter of a mile away, it makes sense that the fishermen right above it were as well. Anyway, the huge scar on the landscape at the chalk pit, was cleverly hidden by a garden finished in 1904 at a cost of almost £400. Originally it was called Holywell Retreat, but in 1922, after paths were cut into the hillside and the beds replanted (in the latest Italianate design) it was renamed the Italian Gardens.

When you pass the Italian Gardens, look at the plain gazebo structure with the slatted wood roof, built into the rising hillside. It looks so plain and irrelevant now, but once that insignificant shack was the most important building in the area. In fact it was of global significance. It is tucked into the right hand side of the gardens and was the terminal building for the Holywell to Dieppe cross-Channel telegraph cable.

Daily messages from Britain to Europe all shot from that building under the Channel. Apparently a telegraph station had also once been at Birling Gap. Most traces of the crucial connection have long been destroyed, but the forgotten building still stands as a little bit of hidden Eastbourne. Legend tells that it was probably at this very spot that the terrible news arrived in June of 1914 of the assassination of Archduke Ferdinand and his wife in Sarejevo, the incident that is said to have triggered World War One.

It does not matter which path you take from this point as they all end up at King Edward's Parade. It is a steep climb back to the main road, so it is not for the faint-hearted! Stop regularly to take in the changing views over the English Channel and, most importantly, smell that beautiful sea air that has drawn visitors here since the time of the Romans.

When you arrive at the top of the path you are back to St Helen's Gardens (once owned by Mrs Helen Reid Stewart) and back to the beginning of our journey. If you walk through the Gardens and look over the railings out to sea below, you will see the tangled overgrown vegetation where an old cottage once stood. It is there that we are going to finish our story.

Sea kale was harvested by our ancestors for millennia and is making a comeback in high class eating establishments.

Here is the chalet where King George V and Queen Mary changed for a dip in 1935.

Here are the Italian Gardens today with little trace of the chalk pit they once were. They were constructed from the old Gore Chalk Pit and survive today much as they were first made. One of the hidden secrets of the gardens is the old terminal building that I am leaning against. It sent and received all messages to and from the continent. It was once one of the most important buildings in the area.

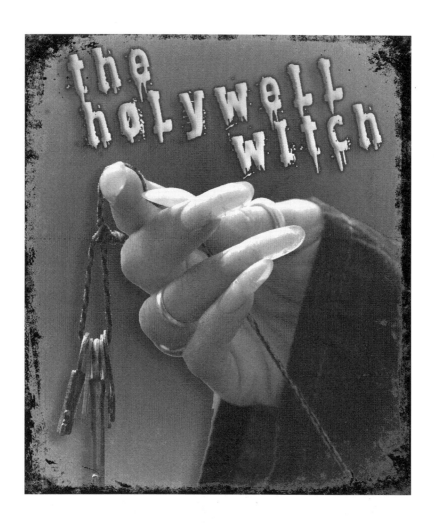

Chapter 21

The Witch!

Well here we are, full circle, almost back to Holywell and the Sugar Loaf, both unique and truly special to Eastbourne. The area has a feel, an aura that is always beautiful and always mysterious. Sometimes the westerly breeze brings all the scents of the wild sea to your nose. You can breathe in an intoxicating mix of Mother Nature at her best and the stunning views simply fill you with a yearning for life. I can see why so many people, including Mother Harriet, found this spot so exhilarating. The white of the cliffs, the blue of the sky, the green hills and ever-changing tides; Holywell is one of the tucked away diamonds of our town.

Now, as I promised at the start, I will polish off this book with the legend of our local witch. Bear in mind these are only the outrageous ramblings of school children, enhanced by our teachers who were probably trying (and failing of course) to keep us away from the ruins of an old cottage near our school. There are even a few facts sprinkled in to the pot!

When I was a boarder at St Bede's, during holidays a few of us stayed on at the school. Throughout these times there was only a skeleton staff. Even better and much to our delight, no lessons. Often a handful of us would escape from the school and go exploring, looking for excitement. One of the places that just had to be reconnoitred was the ruins of the old Weircombe Cottage, hidden down the path to Holywell. The land is now fenced off by high railings and guarded by locked gates, but all the security was terribly inviting to us when we had time on our hands.

The story goes that long ago two sisters lived in the cottage that was hidden away on the edge of the cliffs. One was a famous actress and singer called Winifred Barnes. Born in 1892, by the time she was 16 she was already appearing on the London stage as a chorus girl. Winifred was a classic beauty. In 1909 she appeared in Our Miss Gibbs at the Gaiety Theatre and the owner took her under his wing. George Edwardes was a theatre impresario and put her in several of his plays, leading Winifred to become known as the musical comedy princess of London. During the First World War she also became a bit of a forces sweetheart and it was not long before she caught the eye of a wealthy barrister whom she married. I have failed to find out what happened but at some point she may have taken to farming and cooking! Now, you have to remember most of what I am going to tell you here is little more than hand-me-down gossip.

Somewhere in the early 1920's, Winifred moved into the cottage on the cliff edge at Holywell, mainly because of its superb sea views. It was a little retreat, a bolt hole away from the bright lights, the buzz, and the pressure of the London theatres. Famous actors and writers would visit at her hidden haven. Apparently even Noel Coward was said to pop down to see her.

At some point her elder sister came to live with her and they filled their home with animals, dogs and cats, even parrots.

Gossip went that on occasional days, a large black limousine would be seen quietly slipping down the road to the cottage. Winnie was apparently entertaining a lord! None other the man who invented the flashing pelican crossing lamps, the first Baron Hore-Belisha, of Belisha Beacon fame. His flashing lamps on zebra crossings (which first came into use in the 1930's) must have saved countless lives. He was also the man who brought conscription to the armed forces in 1939. Their little liaisons at Weircombe Cottage caused such a stir amongst the locals that, even years later, a few people would talk about it.

However, late in March of 1935 Winnie became seriously ill and died suddenly a few days later on 5 April. Some say her death was unexplained though it was never investigated. She was only 41. Her sister stayed at the cottage after her death.

Nine years later troops were on manoeuvres before the D-Day Landings in 1944. They were practicing cliff scaling and silently made their way up the chalk at Holywell. Imagine their surprise when they came across Winifred's sister sunbathing naked under the gazeebo behind her cottage! How funny that at the end of our book we come once again to the start, with troops scaling the cliffs.

Winifred's sister lived alone with her animals and slowly went mad. In her final years she would throw abuse, and anything else she could grab, at any passing strangers. If nurses needed to call they would often be accompanied by a police escort to calm her down. At about the same time that I was at St Bede's she broke her hip and needed to be rescued. Rumours at the school were that even her own dogs would sometimes not recognise her and would attack her.

The teachers encouraged the tales of witches to keep us away from the old place (and the sheer drop of the crumbling cliffs beyond it). All their warnings were like flapping a red flag at a young bull. We loved the idea of a crazy old girl chasing us away, even better a witch!

Dares and deeds led to a few of us creeping through the railings and seeking out the old ruins. If we sucked in our bellies real hard, we could just manage to slip through some of the wider ones. Once through we were into a secret world, untouched by other humans. It was like a mini forest on the edge of East-bourne, a truly wild place, left to grow unhindered for decades.

There were rumours that Winifred once used to practice her songs in her garden overlooking the cliffs. When the wind blew a sea mist in from the south, people would say that they could still hear her beautiful ghostly voice hanging on the breeze. Another was that there was a pack of hounds that lived in the house. They would chase children over the edge to their deaths. These tales, so willingly swapped and enhanced by the kids, all made you shiver under your sheets in the dorms (which enticingly overlooked the land where the old cottage stood).

Of course with stories like these we were always on high alert when we went exploring. The pimples were up and the hairs on our little necks stood to attention as we crept closer and closer to the old cottage. It only took one of us to crack and we would all chicken out. Then we would run like crazy things back to the safety of the school. A bird would squawk or a tree branch creak and that was it, just a mad scramble back through the bushes, squishing at high speed through the railings and running for our lives. Safe back at school, bent over breathless, we would laugh our heads off. Not once did we ever make it all the way to the ruins to see the witch!

Anyway the poor old dear died in the early 1970's and that was the end of the Barnes saga…almost. The story of the witches took one final strange twist. After the last sister died the property fell into an even worse state, slowly returning to nature, with trees growing right up to the cottage and ivy creeping up the walls. The once immaculately kept gardens became a wild place for nesting birds, squirrels and rats.

Eventually in 1979, the local council, who were by then responsible for the property, called in demolition experts to pull it down. It was then that I got an excited call from one of my old school mates. "Alex, have you heard?"

"Heard what Paul?"

"They are clearing the site of the old cottage. You know, the haunted one down the path by our old school."

"Oh yeah, I saw some trucks moving up and down there."

"Apparently they have found dozens of items all clearly marked, each one was from an unusual death; a suicide, a fatal car crash, a murder and so on. PLUS, loads of silver stashed under a bed and in that shed that we used to creep past!"

"Well slap my giddy aunt," I laughed.

"I told you there were witches there," he shouted breathlessly down the line. "Gotta go, my dad's picking me up in his taxi at eleven." I was left holding the phone with the dialling tone humming away, staring at the floor, remembering all the times we had dared to creep into the old grounds.

So we have to wonder if all those rumours held a little truth to them after all! Oh my, how we would have scarpered away even faster if we knew what she had been collecting!

This wonderful photo taken by professional 'star' photographer Rita Martin, captures that wide-eyed innocence of Winifred Barnes that the theatre goers loved.

There are only a handful of photos that still exist of Weircombe Cottage. When I was a kid it was already rundown and overgrown with many of the lovely ornaments broken or stolen. There was a wonderful painting on one white-washed side wall of a galleon sailing on a blue sea. Some people called the pretty white painted building Cliffside. Note the older of the two images how there was another substantial building behind the cottage possibly Holywell House. There were also coastguard cottages nearby that were demolished to make way for St Luke's Children's Hospital in 1888. The hospital was in turn replaced by Dolphin Court Flats which survive today in Holywell Cliff Road.

EPILOGUE

Here we are at last. We have finally come to the end of our circular town building tour. After many years I have put all my researching tools and piles of notes away. It is true to say that the Eastbourne we see today was turned, mainly by the ideas of a few men, from little more than outlying hamlets and fishing villages, into one of the premier resorts in Britain. There is little doubt that Eastbourne would have probably become a town without the 7th Duke of Devonshire (along with his greatest collaborator, George Ambrose Wallis) but what they created was the beautiful heart of our superb seaside resort. It is a heart that still beats to this day.

I hope that this story has brought a bit of old Eastbourne to life for you. Maybe one day you may find the time to take a trip along the little path that runs besides Bede's School, down to a special place where fishermen and witches once lived, where a duke dreamt of a new town, and where holy water still pours from the cliffs.

THE END

VISIT AMAZON

TO SEE A LIST OF

ALEX'S CURRENT BOOKS